Two Jews, Three Opinions

Two Jews, Three Opinions

Klal Yisrael, Pluralism,
and the Jewish Community Day School Network

BARBARA SHEKLIN DAVIS

RESOURCE *Publications* · Eugene, Oregon

TWO JEWS, THREE OPINIONS
Klal Yisrael, Pluralism, and the Jewish Community Day School Network

Copyright © 2019 Barbara Sheklin Davis. All rights reserved. Except for brief quotations in critical publications or reviews, no part of this book may be reproduced in any manner without prior written permission from the publisher. Write: Permissions, Wipf and Stock Publishers, 199 W. 8th Ave., Suite 3, Eugene, OR 97401.

Resource Publications
An Imprint of Wipf and Stock Publishers
199 W. 8th Ave., Suite 3
Eugene, OR 97401

www.wipfandstock.com

PAPERBACK ISBN: 978-1-5326-7331-3
HARDCOVER ISBN: 978-1-5326-7332-0
EBOOK ISBN: 978-1-5326-7333-7

Manufactured in the U.S.A.   01/21/19

KLAL YISRAEL

"We believe that the future of the Jewish People is enshrined in the notion of Jewish Peoplehood—Klal Yisrael."
RAVSAK

"Synonym for the Jewish people."
JEWISH PUBLICATION SOCIETY

"The unfractured totality of Jewish existence and the ultimate significance of every single Jew."
CHANCELLOR ISMAR SCHORSCH, THE JEWISH THEOLOGICAL SEMINARY

"Yiddish expression [initially] used as a way of referring to all the religious Jews in the world; however, after the re-emergence of the Zionist movement its meaning changed to refer to all Jews in the world regardless of their religious views and it is now used to promote a sense of community amongst world Jewry regardless of background."
AARDVARK ISRAEL

"Jewish Peoplehood without a specific connection to nationhood."
THE PEOPLEHOOD PAPERS

"Klal Yisrael includes both the yeshiva boys and the Women of the Wall in Jerusalem, the intermarried Jews and Chabadniks in Los Angeles, the totally secular and the totally Satmar in New York."
COFFEE SHOP RABBI

"No matter what you call it, the Jewish people is basically one extended family: not as huge as we could have been had Hitler not done his best to exterminate us; not as powerful as our enemies (and even some of our best friends) believe; not as happy as we should be, nor as dysfunctional as we sometimes ourselves fear. It is a family of roughly 13 million, about half of them living in Israel and the rest spread around the world. As with all families, there are success stories and black sheep (sometimes combined in the same figure). There are the wealthy, the poor, the outstanding and the ordinary. We have the generous and the stingy; the fun and the infuriating. As one of my own relatives likes to point out, you don't always have to like family members, but you have to love them."
LIAT COLLINS, JERUSALEM POST

Contents

Introduction | ix

1. Jewish Day Schools in America | 1
2. A Network Is Born | 9
3. Pluralism and Jewish Community Day Schools | 21
4. The Rise of RAVSAK | 38
5. RAVSAK under New Governance—2010–2016 | 51
6. The Demise of RAVSAK | 62
7. Challenges of the Jewish Community Day School Network | 77
8. Responses to the Challenges | 100
9. Epilogue | 129

Bibliography | 141

Introduction

Rabbi Ishmael and Rabbi Elazar ben Azaria were once staying in the same room. Rabbi Ishmael was lying down and Rabbi Elazar was standing up. When it came time to say the evening Shema, Rabbi Elazar lay down to say the prayer, following the teaching of the House of Shammai about how to say the evening Shema. However, when he did so, Rabbi Ishmael stood up to say it. Afterward Rabbi Elazar said to his companion: "Why are you being so contrary? You have no objections to saying the Shema while lying down." Rabbi Ishmael responded: "I stood up in order to follow the teaching of the House of Hillel. If students were watching us, I did not want them to assume that there was only one correct way.

TALMUD, BERACHOT 11A

JEWS ARE DISPUTATIOUS. WHETHER they debate the nature of Jewish identity, Israeli politics, or the role of women in Judaism, they are unlikely to agree on anything. We all know the story of the shipwrecked Jew who built two synagogues on his island: one to attend and one he would never set foot in. The Talmud [*Eruvin 13b, Gitin 6b*] says, *"Elu ve-elu divrei Elokim hayyim* — These and these are the words of the living God." Disputation, as Susan Glenn puts it, "may be a Jewish cultural habit."[1] "If anything, disunity has been the norm of Jewish history,"[2] writes Steven Bayme. The Jerusalem

---

1. Glenn, "Jewish Cold War," Para. 4.
2. Bayme, *Jewish Arguments*, 343.

INTRODUCTION

Center for Public Affairs declares that "Plural expressions of Judaism have long been a feature of Jewish communal life."[3]

Nowhere is this more evident than in Jewish education. To be a Jew has always meant to be a literate Jew. "No ancient civilization can offer a parallel comparable in intensity with Judaism's insistence upon teaching the young and inculcating in them the traditions and customs of their people,"[4] wrote Mordechai Kaplan, founder of Reconstructionist Judaism. But the definition of Jewish literacy has meant very different things in different eras. In the twenty-first century, there is no more an agreed-upon definition of an educated Jew than there is of who is a Jew.

In the United States, education of the majority of Jewish children has been provided by either day schools or supplementary schools. Full-time Jewish day schools are the subject of *Two Jews, Three Opinions*. The Jewish day school world in the United States is currently in the throes of major change. While Haredi (ultra-Orthodox) schools are experiencing burgeoning enrollment, those that serve the rest of the American Jewish population are facing challenges of demography, affordability, and sustainability. Five major organizations led the field of full-time Jewish education of the non-Haredi young in the twentieth century. PEJE, the Partnership for Excellence in Jewish Education, was an organization focused on enhancing day school leadership and providing financial support for schools. Three were denominationally-based organizations: PARDeS, the Progressive Association of Reform Day Schools; the Conservative movement's Schechter Day School Network; and the Modern Orthodox Yeshiva University School Partnership (YUSP). RAVSAK, the Jewish Community Day School Network, the fifth, was the umbrella network for non-denominational Jewish community day schools. On July 1, 2016, all five of these organizations merged into a new entity called *Prizmah: Center for Jewish Day Schools*.

Why did Modern Orthodox, Conservative, Reform, and Community day school organizations combine under one roof at this particular time? The answer, according to Prizmah, was that while denominational differences were important, issues such as affordability, recruitment, retention, leadership, governance, and professional development were not denominationally dependent and could be addressed across streams. The creation of Prizmah was the fulfillment of the vision of two philanthropic organizations: the AVI CHAI Foundation and the Jim Joseph Foundation. AVI

---

3. Jerusalem Center for Public Affairs, "Statement," Para. 5.
4. Kaplan, *Judaism as Civilization*, 196.

Introduction

CHAI, endowed in 1984 by Zalman Bernstein, a Modern Orthodox *ba'al teshuva* (returnee to the faith), was committed to the perpetuation of the Jewish people, Judaism, and the centrality of the State of Israel to the Jewish people. It had announced its sunset in 2020. The eponymous Jim Joseph Foundation, established in 2006, was devoted exclusively to supporting the Jewish education of youth in the United States. Jim Joseph had made known its contention that the field of Jewish education needed to be unified.

Prizmah planned to offer programs, services, and networking opportunities to the more than 375 Jewish day schools and nearly 100,000 students served by its legacy organizations. Yet Prizmah, which means "prism" in Hebrew, struck some as an odd appellation for an organization seeking to unify divergent educational constituencies, inasmuch as a prism separates light into its distinctive components. Prizmah acknowledged the importance of respecting stream differences and vowed not to homogenize them, but the question for many Jewish educators was whether Prizmah could accomplish what many consider an impossibility: melding Orthodox and non-Orthodox educational sectors into a sustainable enterprise that could service the increasingly diverse field of young Jewish learners in the twenty-first century.

An alternative vision of a unified field existed prior to the creation of Prizmah and is the focus of this book. For thirty-six years, the Jewish Community Day School Network, known by its Hebrew acronym RAVSAK, for *Reshet Batei Sefer K'hilati'im*, had worked to create and sustain a unique Jewish educational paradigm for the changing landscape of American Jewry in the late twentieth and early twenty-first centuries. Community day schools, joining together to enhance and expand their educational philosophy and goals while remaining autonomous and locally-based, developed a model network with a commitment to diversity, pluralism, and *Klal Yisrael*. One of the questions this book seeks to answer is why this model, well-suited to contemporary Jewish America, was not expanded and encouraged.

The Community Day School Network began because the needs of independent Jewish schools for connection could not be met by any of the denominationally-based educational associations in existence in the late twentieth century. The small group of community day schools, specific to their own communities and the people in them, represented, as Marc Kramer has noted,[5] both a return to a traditional mode of schooling, in which a Jewish community established and supported a full day of school

---
5. Kramer, "Teaching," 67–8.

Introduction

for all of its children, and a move toward a new type of school that was post-denominational, co-educational, and egalitarian. Many of these schools operated on the principle of "maximal inclusion," enrolling all Jewish children regardless of their families' level of practice or commitment to Judaism, as well as children of multicultural and multifaith families.

In the words of the community day school movement's founders, the primary purpose of a Jewish communal day school was to serve the Jewish community in which it was located, offering that community the finest Jewish education possible, regardless of affiliation or lack thereof. They declared that such a school must be responsive to, and representative of its community, "excluding none of the various Jewish philosophical and ideological groups of which the community may be composed."[6] This put them at odds with other networks, as they urged the communal school to "exhort the Jewish community at large, its *Klal Yisrael*, to a heightened Jewish consciousness, strengthened identity, and deepened commitment, without delineating dictates of religious ideology or designating preferred religious tenets or philosophical ideals." This openness and acceptance was ahead of its time, and it put community schools at cross purposes with denominational day schools and their respective associations.

The community day school movement, a singularly-purposed segment of the Jewish educational mosaic, has not been studied before. As the contemporary American Jewish community struggles to adjust to rapidly and dramatically changing demographics, affiliations, and identities, it is instructive to see how community day schools and their network anticipated and accommodated many of the twenty-first century's most significant Jewish educational challenges. The origins, philosophy, development, challenges, and accomplishments of the community day school network deserve to be studied comprehensively, utilizing primary sources and firsthand accounts. As head of a community day school and a representative of community day schools and their interests to the RAVSAK boards, I have had the privilege both of being a member and beneficiary of the Jewish Community Day School Network and of recording and participating in much of RAVSAK's governance. The goal of this book is to illuminate the community day school network's distinctive contributions to Jewish education and to discern the factors that led to its success and then its elimination

---

6. This and subsequent quotations and citations are from primary sources in possession of the author and archived at the American Jewish Archives, 3101 Clifton Ave., Cincinnati, OH 45220.

Introduction

as a separate entity, the exceptionality and importance of which was largely undervalued and vastly underserved by most segments of the American Jewish establishment.

I

Jewish Day Schools in America

Here is one astounding constant of Jewish history since (at least) Mishnaic times: every boy was expected to go to school from the age of three to the age of thirteen. This duty was imposed on male children and their parents, administered and often subsidized by the community. At school, often a tiny one-room, one-teacher, multiage affair, the boys studied Hebrew – not their mother tongue, and not a living language even in Talmudic times – at a level sufficient for both reading and writing. This ten-year study was unconditional, independent of class, pedigree, and means.[1]

AMOS OZ

AS JEWS EMIGRATED FROM the Old to the New World, the religious education of their children was on their agenda, but attended to in random fashion. The Sephardic Jews who came first established Jewish schools in the early eighteenth century. Most Jewish education prior to that time had been provided for well-to-do families by private tutors. The Spanish and Portuguese Synagogue, Shearith Israel, opened a school in New York City in 1731 and focused on Hebrew studies, later adding secular subjects. Closed during the Revolutionary War, it reopened as a full-fledged day school, receiving funds from the state and thereby enabling students of lesser means to

---

1. Oz, *jewsandwords*, 7.

receive a Jewish education. A few other, mostly short-lived, Jewish schools opened during the colonial period. They were generally co-educational, dividing as their students reached Judaic maturity, with boys being prepared for bar mitzvah and girls for domestic pursuits.

In the nineteenth century, newly-arrived German Jews established gender-segregated schools, taught in German, with Judaic curricula that adhered to the Reform model, dispensing with ritual and focusing on *midot,* or values. In 1842, New York's first Ashkenazi synagogue, B'nai Jeshurun, established a day school. Other schools were created in Cincinnati and Philadelphia. Like their predecessors, these schools were short-lived. By the end of the nineteenth century, public education had superseded Jewish day school education as both established and immigrant Jewish communities saw it as the gateway to the success in America that they wanted for their children. In 1901, there were only two Jewish day schools in North America. Full-time Jewish education for the young was not on the community's radar, although many boys studied privately in *cheders* (rooms) with rabbis. In 1908, the New York City police commissioner complained that Jewish immigrants were responsible for half of the crime in the city, having a natural propensity for criminal activity. His comments gave rise to a surge of effort to improve Jewish education through structured educational experiences for Jewish youth, whose truancy rates from public school were extremely high. A cadre of Jewish philanthropists and educators, spurred by the police commissioner's remarks, set out to make Jewish education a communal responsibility, with after-school Jewish education, through community Talmud Torahs, complementing public school education.

Thus arose a two-tiered system that would persist for decades: day schools for the Jewish few and afternoon schools for the Jewish many. In 1914, when more than a million and a half Eastern European Jews emigrated to the United States, it was the public school system that was tasked with turning those of school age into Americans. It was left to the one-room *cheders,* Talmud Torahs (supplementary religious schools), and the day schools to keep them Jewish. By 1935, eighteen Jewish day schools had been founded, described as "old-type Yeshibah," "modern-type Yeshibah," and "private progressive-type"[2] by Israel Chipkin. He also disparaged them as institutions for the select because "they are financially prohibitive to the masses and cannot readily become the typical community school."[3]

2. Chipkin, *Twenty-Five Years,* 59.
3. Chipkin, *Twenty-Five Years,* 59.

Although Chipkin believed that there would continue to be "a sufficiently interested minority within the community who will make every sacrifice to maintain them" and expected these schools to "supply that contingent of intensively trained Jewish youth who enter our higher schools of Jewish learning," he concluded that they "must always remain the opportunity of the exclusive few."[4]

Still, by the middle of the twentieth century, the number of day schools had climbed to thirty-five, enrolling 7,700 students in seven states and Canadian provinces. Most of these schools were Orthodox and were primarily for boys, although some separate schools were established for girls. The growth in Orthodox Jewish day schools was driven in large measure by Holocaust survivors who arrived in the United States with no desire to emulate the assimilationist goals of previous immigrants. They preferred to send their sons to yeshivas to study Talmud and rabbinical literature and their daughters to Bais Yaakov schools to learn *Tanakh* (bible) and *dinim u minhagim* (laws and customs). Secular studies were a decidedly secondary consideration.

Torah Umesorah (Torah and Tradition), the National Society for Hebrew Day Schools, was created in 1944 to foster and promote Torah-based Jewish religious education in North America. Its founders envisioned a network of dual-curriculum Orthodox day schools that would provide Judaic education for half the day and secular education for the second half. Each school was headed by an ordained rabbi who served as principal or headmaster and a general studies principal, preferably a Torah-observant Jew, who was responsible for a secular studies program that corresponded to the public school curriculum.

After World War II, the Jewish educational world underwent profound changes, reflective of residential shifts. As Jews moved from crowded urban neighborhoods to sprawling suburbs and built new houses of worship, congregational schools began to supersede community Talmud Torahs. Within the general Jewish community there were serious misgivings about day schools, chief among them that day schools would jeopardize the integration of Jewish children into American society. Day school proponents were considered, in William W. Brickman's words, to be of "old-world background, financially underdeveloped, outlandish in appearance and inarticulate in the language of the land."[5] Day schools were seen as having

---

4. Chipkin, *Twenty-Five Years*, 59.
5. Brickman, "American," 176.

inadequate facilities and outdated pedagogy. "Gray within and without"[6] was the description applied by Mary Antin in 1912.

But there was a downside to acceptance in the larger society, as noted by Alvin Schiff in *The Jewish Day School in America*: "It has enabled the Jew to live freely as a Jew, with all that his Jewishness might imply. At the same time, it has enabled him to lose, without pain or difficulty, all signs of his Jewishness, and to disappear into the growing, mingling crowds."[7] Many in the Jewish community had begun a reappraisal of the price paid by those who had held Americanization as their primary goal in the twentieth century. The Pluralism Project phrased it well: "In the United States, Jews have found a degree of social acceptance unparalleled in their long history. But the openness of American society has proven to be a double-edged sword. While American Jews experience unprecedented opportunity for advancement and inclusion, they also face the challenge of ever-diminishing numbers and the fear of extinction as an identifiable group."[8]

As a result of this awareness, proponents of day school education began to make some headway by the mid-century. Emanuel Gamoran, Director of Education at the Union of American Hebrew Congregations, declared in 1950, "We must admit that there is a great need for the training of Jewish leadership of which Hebraic education is a basis. We have no such basis now in the ranks of Reform Judaism. Without it we shall be largely dependent on Orthodox and Conservative Jews to supply us with children who have a sufficient Hebraic background to go into Jewish work, into Jewish education, or into the rabbinate."[9] While it was not uncommon for non-Orthodox families to send their children to Orthodox institutions, day school advocates within the Conservative and Reform movements began laying the groundwork for their own schools. They argued that only a truly intensive but non-Orthodox Jewish education could prepare future leaders for their movements, especially in a post-Holocaust world that no longer had European Jewry to provide an intellectual and cultural elite.

In 1951, the Beth El Day School in Rockaway Park, New York became the first day school to be sponsored by a Conservative synagogue. The first school to adopt the name of Solomon Schechter, founder of the Conservative movement in the United States, was the Solomon Schechter School of

---

6. Antin, *Promised Land*, 80.
7. Schiff, *Jewish Day School*, 4.
8. Pluralism Project, "Challenge," Para. 1.
9. Gamoran cited in Sheramy, "Tuition," Para. 8.

Queens, which opened in 1956. "The growth of the day school will help the Conservative movement to create a reservoir of intensely educated and deeply dedicated men and women,"[10] stated the United Synagogue Commission on Jewish Education in 1958. Under the aegis of the Conservative movement, other day schools were founded, and in 1965 the Association of Solomon Schechter Day Schools was created to promote "the continued growth and vitality of its member schools, which serve a broad Jewish population and are characterized by Conservative thought and practice, achievement and social responsibility, in a culture of joyous spiritual engagement, caring and community."[11] Schechter schools had autonomy in most policy areas as long as all matters pertaining to religious practice and observance were aligned with the essential understandings of Conservative Judaism.

Still, most mid-century Jewish parents simply did not regard day schools as a necessary or even a viable educational option. Statements like those of Gamoran and the United Synagogue Commission on Jewish Education notwithstanding, most postwar Reform and Conservative Jews had profound misgivings about an educational system that threatened to undermine the hard-sought integration of Jews into the wider American social fabric through the public school system.

Then things began to change again. By the mid-1960s, the growth of the Orthodox community, the concern for Jewish survival after the Holocaust and the creation of the State of Israel, as well as growing disenchantment with the public school system and a new sense of Jewish ethnic pride, resulted in growth in the day school movement. By 1964, there were 306 Jewish day schools in North America, enrolling 65,400 students, or nine percent of children enrolled in some form of Jewish education in the United States. Most of these schools had been founded under the auspices of the Torah Umesorah movement.

Another factor coming into play was the concept of cultural pluralism. Although *E Pluribus Unum* remained the national motto of the United States, the meaning and worthiness of assimilation was increasingly questioned in the second half of the twentieth century. Those who once unhesitatingly accepted and championed Americanization and assimilation were challenged by others who saw class, race, ethnicity, and diversity as positive values that deserved to be fostered in a multicultural society.

---

10. United Synagogue, cited in Ackerman, "Strangers," 92–3.
11. United Synagogue, cited in Ackerman, "Strangers," 92–3.

The term "cultural pluralism" was coined by the American Jewish philosopher, Horace Kallen, who rejected the dominant paradigm of America as a melting pot in favor of an orchestral metaphor. Kallen saw American civilization as the "perfection of the cooperative harmonies" of European civilization in what he called "an orchestration of mankind."[12] As in an orchestra, he explained, "every type of instrument has its specific timbre and tonality, founded in its substance and form; as every type has its appropriate theme and melody in the whole symphony, so in society each ethnic group is the natural instrument, its spirit and culture are its theme and melody, and the harmony and dissonances and discords of them all make the symphony of civilization, with this difference: a musical symphony is written before it is played; in the symphony of civilization the playing is the writing, so that there is nothing so fixed and inevitable about its progressions as in music, so that within the limits set by nature they may vary at will, and the range and variety of the harmonies may become wider and richer and more beautiful."[13]

Kallen and Reconstructionist leader Mordechai Kaplan saw America as a mosaic of cultures, in which peoples of all nationalities, religions, and cultural traditions would retain their distinctiveness but also participate fully in American society. Jews could exist therein as a discrete community, but would not be unique or alone in doing so, and their religious/ethnic/cultural identification would be purely voluntary. In their eyes, pluralistic Judaism was non-denominational and unaffiliated with any organization or umbrella. It did not subscribe to the tenets of any movement but instead was open to the beliefs of all movements. The phrase bandied about was "Labels are for jars, not Jews."

Thus in 1978 the United Synagogue Commission on Jewish Education expressed the goals of the Schechter schools in a way that made clear that it was forsaking the immigrant experience in favor of a forward-looking American Jewishness with a positive view of difference: "The whole point of studying in the religious school is to learn what makes the Jew different . . . and to make a decision as to why you should be different."[14] In 1985, the Reform movement's Union of American Hebrew Congregations reversed its longstanding opposition to day schools and voted to support the establishment of Reform day schools, joining a movement that by then had

---

12. Kallen, "Democracy," Para. 45.
13. Kallen, "Democracy," Para. 45.
14. United Synagogue, cited in Ackerman, "Strangers," 92–3.

reached 500 Jewish day schools across the country (the majority of which were still Orthodox).

As intermarriage rates increased and research on Jewish day schools began to emerge, the public discourse began to change. When Alvin Schiff published *The Jewish Day School in America* in 1966, he concluded unequivocally that "the Jewish Day School has demonstrated convincingly that it is the best way of combatting the corrosive effects of assimilation. It has become the most effective instrument for transmitting the Jewish heritage to Jewish youth, and consequently the surest method of insuring American Jewry's creative continuity and ability to enrich American life."[15]

The day schools that existed in the middle of the twentieth century were of many different kinds and adhered to a variety of religious practices. The majority, which were Orthodox in orientation and located in large urban centers, did not meet the needs of Jewish families in smaller Jewish communities for reasons that included both geography and ideology. The same was true for schools sponsored by denominations. Yet despite the fact that most American Jewish families were still firmly committed to the public school system as the engine of both personal success and national cohesion, a new kind of day school began to develop organically: the Jewish community day school.

Across the United States and Canada, Jewish communal leaders began to recognize that they had an uncommon mission, reflective both of the historical role of the Jewish community in the education of its youth and of the increasing diversity of North American Jewry. They also realized that they had a common mission. Working in isolation from one another, without a professional umbrella, made their task more arduous. Absent a national organization for community day schools, there was no way these schools could share philosophies, goals, ideas, curricula, methodologies, textbook lists, approaches to teaching Judaism from a pluralistic standpoint, problems, challenges, and successes. Daniel W. Bennett, director of Jewish Studies at the Theodor Herzl Jewish Day School in Denver, Colorado, wrote "Schools in existence from ten, twelve, even eighteen years, had not been aware that other schools shared their philosophy, that Jews in many communities had sensed the need to establish community day schools."[16]

---

15. Schiff, *Jewish Day School*, 249.
16. Bennett, "Community," 14.

Around the country, schools were working in isolation, reinventing the wheel and feeling that something was missing.

That realization led to a milestone gathering in 1980 at which a groundswell begat a formal movement.

2

A Network Is Born

In striving to achieve excellence in Jewish education and to encourage all community members to avail themselves of its educational services, the communal school must approach Judaism, in all aspects of Jewish practice and modes of thought, with reverence, respect, and without prejudice, regardless of the specific practices of the school.

PHILOSOPHY STATEMENT OF THE JCDSN 1980[1]

IN JUNE OF 1980, a group of like-minded day school educators from eight different communities met in Cincinnati, Ohio, to create a non-ideological day school association with the goals of striving for excellence in Jewish education for *Klal Yisrael*, heightening Jewish consciousness, strengthening Jewish identity, and deepening Jewish commitment. They developed deeply-felt and strongly-worded statements of philosophy, which, even decades later, clearly illuminate the issues that led to the founding of the new network.

Aware that "an association which transcends particularistic ideologies and embraces all phases and abiding values of Judaism has not heretofore existed for communal schools," they declared it "propitious, given the present conditions and need for mutual counsel and interaction, that we,

---

1. This and subsequent quotations and citations are from primary sources in possession of the author and archived at the American Jewish Archives, 3101 Clifton Ave., Cincinnati, OH 45220.

sharing common goals and objectives, gather as an association hereafter known as the Association of Jewish Communal Day Schools (AJCDS)." They explained that the day school movement had undergone extensive growth and that ideologically-based schools and others belonging to Torah Umesorah and the Lubavitch movement had formed commissions "to provide strength and services for their constituent schools to insure the continuity of their respective orientations." They sought a similar organizational structure to provide mutual cooperation and reciprocal assistance among members for schools not affiliated with ideological or interest groups.

The initial meeting was attended by representatives from geographically diverse communities: Toledo, Cleveland, and Cincinnati, Ohio; Plantation, Florida; Winnipeg, Manitoba; Pittsburgh, Pennsylvania; Birmingham, Alabama, and Louisville, Kentucky. Another dozen schools expressed interest in the association but were unable to attend the meeting. Illana Sebo, chair of the group's ad hoc steering committee, sent a mailing to those schools that defined the rationale, philosophy, objectives, membership requirements, and services the organization proposed to provide. Sebo noted that the papers were intended for presentation to the boards of the schools for preliminary approval and asked each board to send one representative to the lay Board of AJCDS, from which an executive working committee would be selected. The lay board, together with the steering committee, was to meet to further develop the organization of the association and to begin providing some of the services.

On July 15, 1980, the new Association of Jewish Communal Day Schools sent a letter to colleagues in unaffiliated schools throughout the United States, telling them about the results of the meeting held in Cincinnati and including three papers, developed for approval by the boards of day schools committed in the new organization. The papers delineated rationale, philosophy, and objectives of the AJCDS and defined membership and services. Noting that the creation of a new national organization was a formidable undertaking, the group set member fees of one hundred dollars per school and 50 cents per student and explained that it was receiving support from the American Association for Jewish Education.

Membership requirements for Association schools clearly defined the way the new organization differed from similar entities: "Membership shall be open to any Jewish day school whose objectives, philosophy, and policies are compatible with those adumbrated in the AJCDS statement of philosophy. Such a compatibility can exist only with those schools wherein: the governing body of the school is representative of all segments of the Jewish community at large; the governing body of the school is free to develop its own policies for every phase of the school's scope of operations and implementations of its services in response to the needs of its community; the school approaches all modes of Jewish thought and practice with respect and without prejudice, regardless of the specific practice of the school."

Services that the AJCDS proposed to provide, some through the offices of the American Association for Jewish Education, included communication, in-service education, consultation, placement, legal aid, resource and data banks, and aid in opening new schools. The overall intent was to assist all communal day schools in achieving excellence. Specifically, the organization proposed to help with communication, in-service education, consultation, legal aid, resource and data banks, evaluation systems, placement and human resources, curricula, integration of Judaic and general studies, access to national and local educational resources, public relations, evaluation and visitation, and budgeting and fundraising.

The next opportunity for those interested in community day school education to meet occurred in August 1986, when a mini-conference for community day schools, sponsored by the Jewish Education Services of North America (JESNA), was convened at the Coalition for the Advancement of Jewish Education (CAJE) Conference at the University of Maryland. The mini-conference was designed to give principals and others an opportunity to discuss areas of common interest and their unique needs. The full-day session was attended by more than two dozen community day school principals, as well as a number of teachers, bureau directors, and guests.

While most of the sessions were informational and designed for the exchange of information, the highlight was chair Barbara Steinberg's keynote address, which identified the challenges and issues faced by community day school principals. Although the complete text of Steinberg's talk has been lost, an article in the March 13, 1987 *Jewish Floridian of Palm Beach County* contains an accounting of some of her points. She was quoted as saying, "The responsibility to teach ideology should be left to the home and synagogue. The school should teach ritual and ethical behavior. I believe that we have to respect parents as having made intelligent decisions about the way they wish to conduct the religious life of their families." Steinberg also noted that in community day schools, which by their very nature enrolled students from diverse Jewish backgrounds, beliefs, and practices, it was the goal of the Jewish studies curriculum to "teach a religious philosophy that begins with tolerance and will ultimately lead to appreciation, then acceptance, and finally to admiration of the differences as well as the commonalities among the Jewish people."

Mini-conference participants scheduled a meeting to further discuss the concept and development of a community day school network. A planning committee began to develop a formal network conference to be held in January 1987. It was agreed that a newsletter would serve as a very important communication vehicle and plans called for the first issue to appear in December.

Another new network shared its natal date with the JCDSN, the Jewish Community High School Network or JCHSN. Sharing parentage with JESNA, the JCHSN proudly announced "A Network is Born!" The press release explained that due to a resurgence of interest in community high schools, a Jewish Community High School Network had been formed to encourage cooperation and coordination of Jewish high schools which were sponsored by local federations and governed by an autonomous board or by a subcommittee of the board of the sponsoring federation, bureau of Jewish education, or college of Jewish studies that represented the constituency of the school and the community at large. Unlike congregational or intercongregational schools, community high schools were financed by federation allocations, tuition fees, and sometimes per capita contributions by congregations for their members' children. The new network included schools from 26 states, Canada and Argentina, and hoped to convene meetings once a year. With assistance from JESNA, it planned to publish a newsletter for the creative exchange of ideas on issues such as administration, personnel recruitment, development, and retention, curricular and extracurricular materials, finances, and working with parents and lay boards.

Back at the JCDSN, there was considerable discussion concerning the need to clarify what was meant by a "community day school." For the purpose of the miniconference, community schools had been defined by JESNA as schools which had no affiliation with any denominational group, i.e., Torah Umesorah, Solomon Schechter Day School Association, Union of American Hebrew Congregations, The National Commission on Torah Education of Yeshiva University, and United Synagogue of America. Schools formally affiliated or having ongoing contact with any of these organizations did not come under the rubric of community day school for the purpose of the mini-conference. It was agreed that ultimately, in questionable cases, principals would clarify their status with their school boards. For the upcoming conference, it was decided to utilize the same definition for non-affiliated schools used for the mini-conference, regardless of how the school was listed; some felt, however, that Network membership should be restricted to non-affiliated community day schools that had a clear-cut transideological and pluralistic approach. The issue was placed on the conference agenda. Also on the agenda was the question of membership: Was the network for schools or principals, professionals or lay leaders, or all of the above? Initially, it was agreed to view the group as a fellowship of principals.

In the spring of 1987, JESNA announced that a Jewish Community Day School Network for community day schools had been officially created at an historic conference held in West Palm Beach, Florida. The Network was established, the announcement read, "with the encouragement of the Jewish Education Service of North America, Inc. (JESNA), and was designed to give non-affiliated day schools throughout the United States and Canada an opportunity to share and exchange ideas, budgets, curricular and other materials, and to discuss the common ideology which links community schools." The announcement further clarified that "Member schools are either independent or communally sponsored, receive Federation support, and embrace a pluralistic approach to transmitting the Jewish heritage and values in their educational programs. The schools are committed to a set of principles which represent an ideological model for transideological Jewish education. They acknowledge the validity of all major streams of Jewish thought, and the incorporation of this principle into the curricula of community day schools. This acknowledgement implies that there exist many possible options for the expression of Judaism. In addition, the group underscored the importance or showing appreciation and advocacy for the value concept of *Klal Yisrael* and promotion or participation in Jewish community life. The Network leaders hope to improve the effectiveness of Jewish community day schools by: defining, clarifying and advocating common areas of interest; facilitating the professional growth of administrators and staff; providing professional and personal support for administrators and staff; and facilitating the development of lay leadership."

The founding schools included in the network were:

    Abraham Joshua Heschel Day School (New York, New York)
    Agnon School (Cleveland, Ohio)
    Akiba Hebrew Academy (Dallas, Texas)

Akiva Academy (Youngstown, Ohio)

B'nai Shalom Synagogue Day School (Greensboro, North Carolina)

Brandeis/Hillel Day School Community Day School (San Francisco, California)

Community Hebrew Academy (Savannah, Georgia)

El Paso Hebrew Day School (El Paso, Texas)

Eliahu Academy (Louisville, Kentucky)

Fort Worth Hebrew Day School (Fort Worth, Texas)

Hebrew Academy of Tidewater (Virginia Beach, Virginia)

Hebrew Day School of Central Florida (Maitland, Florida)

Heritage Academy (Longmeadow, Massachusetts)

Weiner Jewish Secondary School (Houston, Texas)

Jewish Community Day School of West Palm Beach (Palm Beach Gardens, Florida)

Jewish Community Junior High School (La Jolla, California)

Jewish Day School of Metro Seattle (Seattle, Washington)

Jewish Day School of San Antonio (San Antonio, Texas)

Kinneret Day School (Bronx, New York)

Lancaster Jewish Day School (Lancaster, Pennsylvania)

Max Gilbert Hebrew Academy (Syracuse, New York)

Milwaukee Jewish Day School (Milwaukee, Wisconsin)

N. Peninsula Jewish Community Day School (Foster City, California)

Portland Jewish Academy (Portland, Oregon)

Shalom Day School (Sacramento, California)

Tehiyah Day School (El Cerrito, California)

Theodor Herzl Jewish Day School (Denver, Colorado)

Tikvah Jewish Day School (Austin, Texas)

Tucson Hebrew Academy (Tucson, Arizona

The first officers of the organization were Chair Barbara Steinberg and Secretary/Treasurer Natalie Berman, and the following committee chairs were appointed: Communications: Daniel Bennett; Events: Frederick Nathan; Resources: Jay Welner; Outreach: Rabbi Jim Rogozen. In addition, four regional coordinators were named to provide information to schools in different areas of the country: Northeast: Rosalee Redelheim; Southwest: Dr. Tamar Saposhnik; Northwest: Rabbi Jim Rogozen; Southeast: Burt Lowlicht; Central States: David Brusin; Canada: Miriam Maltz.

A Network Is Born

On June 30, 1987, Rabbi Rogozen, principal of the Shalom School in Sacramento, California, sent a letter to community day school principals inviting their schools to become charter members of the newly formed Jewish Community Day School Network. He explained that "Our organization, founded with the help of JESNA, is made up of Day Schools which have no particular affiliation with any of the denominational groups in North America (i.e. Reform, Conservative, Reconstructionist or Orthodox). There are more than 20 schools in our Network and we hope to add another 50 in the coming year. The purpose of the JCDSN is to improve the effectiveness of community day schools by: a) defining, clarifying, and advocating common areas of interest; b) facilitating the professional growth of our administrators and staffs; c) providing professional and personal support for our administrators and staffs; d) facilitating the development of lay leadership. The cost of becoming a charter member school is $25 plus $1.00 for every student enrolled in your school (includes preschool). These fees help us bring you our newsletter, our resource materials and specialists, regional workshops and our annual conference."

By June 1987, the Association had published its first eight-page newsletter, held its first network meeting and was making plans for its next conference to be held in Boston in association with the ASCD conference. Sessions at the conference specific to the network included "Does Community Mean Parve?," "Philosophy of Community Day Schools," and "An Appreciation and Acceptance of the Diversity of the Jewish Community."

With the encouragement of JESNA, a group of sixteen educators met to draft documents that would allow for the creation of an incorporated, tax exempt organization to be known as "The Jewish Community Day School Network (JCDSN), with a handwritten translation and abbreviation in Hebrew: *Reshet Batei Sefer K'hilati'im* (RVS'K). This document became known as The Palm Beach Working Paper. Thus was RAVSAK born. Daniel Bennett, who served as communications chair and newsletter editor, recalled that RAVSAK school representatives came to Jewish education with varied backgrounds, interests, and strengths, but were "united in the vision of the importance of our movement: to provide Jewish children from diverse backgrounds and beliefs the opportunity to study together, to learn about and respect each other and to acquire the ability to make informed choices about their own Jewish beliefs and practices."[2] He further clarified that "while the vision is shared by all RAVSAK schools, each is free to

2. Bennett, "Network," 15.

implement it, in its own way. RAVSAK does not intend to set policy for its member schools; each school retains autonomy in all matters of practice and curriculum. RAVSAK is a network of schools which share a philosophy of Jewish pluralism. True to that philosophy, our practices may differ."

The JCDSN, as it was still known (because it didn't require as much explanation as did the RAVSAK acronym) was comprised of Jewish community day schools "which are not affiliated with a particular Jewish denominational movement" and committed to "the acknowledgement of the validity of all major streams of Jewish thought and the incorporation of this principle into their curricula." It was further noted that this implied that there were many possible options for the expression of Judaism. Other guiding principles of the organization were the appreciation of and advocacy for the value concept of *Klal Yisrael* and the promotion of participation in Jewish community life. Dialogue and exchange of ideas, and a willingness to learn from each other, as well as "striving to develop a program which fosters appreciation of the commonalities and differences in Jewish life," rounded out the organization's founding values.

An executive committee structure was established and policies were promulgated regarding *kashrut* at all events, the prohibition of any business or other activities on Shabbat, and the establishment of an annual conference to coincide with a major educational conference. The executive committee was kept busy with activities relating to membership, conference, dues collection, and coordination with other organizations. In 1988, they approved protocols for what was fast becoming an autonomous and well-received conference. By the end of the decade, the JCDSN had published two issues of its newsletter, had begun to use the name RAVSAK, and had announced a new vehicle for sharing ideas across the network, to be called "RAVSAK Schools Update." The early newsletters were compiled and mimeographed or Xeroxed or sometimes even printed for limited distribution to the membership. They contained conference updates, information about new members, school profiles, articles about issues of concern to schools, and congratulatory messages.

The matter of *Klal Yisrael* was very much on the minds of the network founders. At an early conference, a session was devoted to the topic. It defined *Klal Yisrael* in the day school setting as including the common destiny of the people of Israel regardless of the country of residence and historical background; all Jewish people regardless of country of origin; all Jewish people regardless of religious affiliation and observance. It defined a true pluralistic setting as being an environment in which all Jews are welcome; an environment in which Judaism is taught non-hyphenated as a diversified religious civilization; a setting that affirms every Jewish expression and identity not as a starting point to another level of observance, but as a mature premediated choice based on well thought-out personal philosophy and life experiences.

The session affirmed the unity of Judaism but raised the following questions: Is Jewish diversity in conflict with Jewish unity? Does a teacher who is passionately committed to a certain Judaic expression/belief have a role to play in a pluralistic school? What are some of the commonalities of Judaism? Is prayer a unifying experience? Is Jewish study a unifying experience? Is tzedakah a unifying Jewish experience?

When planning for another conference, the officers indicated that they wished to have the following topics addressed at a sharing session: *kashrut, tefillah, kippot*, dress codes, sensitivity to traditional families, Shabbat programming, teaching Shabbat observances, *dinim*/laws, definition of community day schools, sex education, who is a Jew, admission policies and screening, rabbinic involvement, and discussing roots or Jewish history with children of non-Jewish parents. These issues were very critical to the schools in the network. On several occasions the idea of a joint conference with the Schechter network or Torah Umesorah was raised, but the other organizations were not receptive to it. Only JESNA seemed to be supportive of the community school network.

By 1990, there were thirty-eight JCDSN schools. Per capita dues had increased from fifty cents to $1.25 and there was a lot of discussion about outreach and public relations. The format and timing of the newsletter was a matter of fiscal concern even though JESNA was paying the mailing costs, the affiliation of denominational schools, the need to revise the by-laws, and the creation of an information packet for outreach purposes and the conference and its nature, location, and participation preoccupied the executive committee. Former JCDSN Chair Dr. Harvey Raben recalled that, "As school heads, we enjoyed each other's company. We had many common concerns, financial religious and curricular. Operating a pluralistic day school was not simple and the conditions and demographics of a school in Youngstown, Ohio and one in San Francisco were clearly different. Day schools, however, were growing and forming everywhere. Soon there were people coming to our conference from Brooklyn, Washington DC, Charlotte, North Carolina, Austin, Texas and Oklahoma. We all believed that we could learn from one another. Some of the heads had expertise in Hebrew and Judaics and others were general studies specialists. We often discussed whether we were creating Jewish day schools or private schools for Jewish children. During those years we also began to realize that turnover of school heads was preventing us from reaching our full potential. We also felt that we needed a dedicated professional leader and facilitator for our organization once JESNA stepped aside and wished us success on our own."[3]

"RAVSAK goes International" read the headline in the 1990 newsletter, as the interdenominational Toronto Bialik Hebrew Day School was welcomed into the network. The newsletter featured an article about marketing, and the conference included speakers on marketing and advertising, teacher certification, and Bible curriculum. As the network grew, it became apparent that the volunteer leadership, themselves heads of schools, could not do all the work of the burgeoning organization. Ada Michaels, a recently retired head of school, was hired as an administrative consultant. In 1991, the network held its conference in Israel. In that same year, the Jim Joseph Foundation gave RAVSAK a grant of $60,000 to pursue a curriculum proposal focusing on Shabbat, with appropriate philosophy and teaching strategies.

A sharing session at the 1991 conference was very indicative of the nature of the concerns that preoccupied community day school heads and the different ways they dealt with common issues. Topics were admissions policies and screening, the wearing of *kippot* by students and staff, tuition and scholarships, rabbinical involvement, community outreach, and the teaching of *dinim* (laws). (Minutes of the session reveal that the same conversations with the same words could easily take place today.) The Jewish Community Day School Network/RAVSAK continued to grow and expand its programming. Its conferences began to offer board development workshops and attract lay leaders. Dov Bear, the network's traveling teddy, visited classrooms in member schools to keep them in touch with one another and to give children a chance to learn about the Network. The newsletter included professional and curricular development articles and urged members to call one another about school-related matters.

In 1997, the network decided to commit RAVSAK to long-term thinking by undertaking a strategic planning process to sort out what was really important to RAVSAK, focusing on pragmatic implementation. In making the announcement in the JCDSN newsletter, Chair Laurence

---

3. Harvey Raben, email to the author.

A Network Is Born

Kutler wrote, "We are in the business of instilling long term Jewish values in young children which will serve them well as adult members of the Jewish community. No less important is long term thinking for our organization. This is a goal worthy of commitment." The plan was to include goals and action plans for serving as an advocate and support for schools, providing development opportunities for heads of schools, teachers and lay leaders, networking, technology, special education, outreach, public relations, and the conference. The executive committee structure was revised to include regional coordinators as well as a staff liaison coordinator.

By the end of the year, the executive committee had received approval from the membership for a new mission statement: "The Jewish Community Day School Network is an association of Jewish community day schools committed to providing superior education in intensive, pluralistic Jewish learning environments. The Network is a forum for sharing resources, ideas and solutions, enabling the members to draw strength from the diversity and experience of one another to achieve their goals." The Network, the committee declared, "will serve as an advocate and support for its constituencies; provide development opportunities for heads of school, teachers and lay leadership; compile and distribute relevant information on topics such as administration, curriculum, budgeting and finance, fundraising, and recruitment; create and distribute a resource directory; present the yearly conference on topics generated by member schools; share employment information and needs" and finally, "study and pray together to constitute ourselves as a learning community."

In the fall of 1999, Network Chair Karen Feller was able to write a positive report for the membership. She celebrated a resurgence of Jewish day school education across the country and the growth of the Jewish Community Day School Network. "New schools are sprouting up all over the country, and our existing community day schools are growing and adding middle school and high school divisions to their already successful elementary schools." Feller noted that the executive committee consisted of a diverse group of experienced educators and administrators who were dedicated to Jewish education and the enhancement and growth of the community day school movement. She cited many of the network's accomplishments: curriculum ideas, textbook suggestions, models of integration for a dual curriculum, scheduling support, administrative designs, and guidance in recruitment and retention. Most important, she wrote, were the connections the JCDSN provided for Jewish community day school leaders, the comradery, and the ability to discuss "your needs, joys, and frustrations" with others having similar experiences, concerns and needs. She emphasized the value of the network conferences that not only allowed the leaders to serve as resources for one another, but to have access to "the educational leaders who are having the greatest impact on schools today."

Finally, Feller announced that in response to this growth and success of the community day school world, the executive committee had voted to create a national office to meet the demands of both established and new community day schools. At the end of the century, there were sixty member schools representing 10,690 students, a gain of 1,700 students from the previous year. Ada Michaels was promoted to executive director and a national office was established at the United Jewish Federation of Tidewater in Virginia Beach, Virginia.

3

Pluralism and Jewish Community Day Schools

Understanding might lead to tolerance, tolerance to sympathy, sympathy to pluralism, and pluralism, the notion that there was more than one way to legitimately exist as a Jew, to an erosion of their own way of life.

SAMUEL HEILMAN[1]

THE ISSUE OF MULTIPLE perspectives and interpretations has beset Jewry and Jewish educators for generations. Scholars have always debated the *p'shat*, or literal meaning of a text, versus the *drash*, or homiletical meaning. The sages Hillel and Shammai held opposing views on ritual practice, ethics, and theology. A *midrash* (commentary) says that the Torah has seventy faces, indicative of the many valid interpretations of its wisdom. The Talmud presents all sides of a disputation.

The "-isms"—pluralism, relativism, denominationalism—were dominant sources of contention in the post-World War II American Jewish world, particularly as they impacted Jewish education. But when Horace Kallen declared that Jews were "the most successful in eliminating the removable differences between themselves and their social environment"

---

1. Heilman, *Defenders*, 347–8.

because "even their religion is flexible,"[2] he crossed a dangerous line. His contention that Jewish identity was based on culture rather than religion disturbed many. Likewise, pluralistic assertions that there could not be a single explanatory system to account for all the phenomena of life, and relativism's assertion that truth, knowledge, and morality were not absolute but existed in relation to society and history, were nothing short of anathema to many in the Jewish world.

At the same time, educator Judah Pilch and others expressed the belief that even as Jews became acculturated, suburbanized, and accepted in America, "religion, now as ever, was the beginning and the end, of our very life and the length of our days."[3] Sociologist Will Herberg argued in his influential 1955 work, *Protestant, Catholic, Jew*, that religion was the only lasting dimension of culture and the foundation of American pluralism. He stated that all ethnic groups eventually lose their separate identity and replace it with religious community. As the nation, and the Jewish community, moved away from embracing the melting pot theory of Americanization, in which all groups strove to achieve what Daniel Greene called "Anglo-conformity,"[4] the theory of multiculturalism began to infuse the discourse. Multiculturalism allowed for more diverse ways of belonging to the national identity, and did not require any group to give up its history, culture, traditions, or religion as the price of belonging. In fact, the success of the pluralists was such that being different could suddenly be considered "the very essence of being American."[5]

Multiculturalism did not make things easier for day schools, however. Though they could no longer be criticized for being un-American by being Jewish, both day schools and the Jewish community at large had to confront issues that resulted from the divisions within Judaism itself. In 1984, Canadian rabbi Reuven Bulka presciently described the increasing polarization of North American Jewish life, writing that "This is probably the first time that Judaism has been so polarized that today it is not enough to identify oneself by saying one is Jewish. One needs to place a defining adjective in front of that label, and to clearly state whether one is Orthodox, Conservative, Reform or other, of which there are endless possibilities."[6]

2. Kallen, "Democracy," Para. 35.
3. Pilch, cited in Drachler, *Bibliography*, 352.
4. Greene, *Origins*, 184.
5. Greene, *Origins*, 184.
6. Bulka, *Cataclysm*, 43.

Bulka believed that "If unity because of diversity is not possible, unity in spite of diversity should ideally still be achievable."[7] He proposed areas of convergence that would allow "the broad smorgasbord of Jewish tradition in its unadulterated pristine beauty" to be offered to the Jewish community by Orthodox, Conservative, and Reform working together, launching "a massive assault on the main problem facing them squarely in the eye, namely the ignorance and indifference of a great percentage of North America's Jews."[8]

Bulka's dream of an Orthodox-Conservative-Reform alliance went unfulfilled, no doubt due to what Rabbi Walter Wurzburger described in the very foreword to Bulka's book: "Well-intentioned pleas to embark on all-out efforts to assure our survival as one people will hardly be of any avail. What divides us are not only ideological differences but irreconcilable conflicts about the nature of Jewish identity and status . . . The difficulties arise not from institutional concerns, parochialism, or lack of good will, but reflect fundamental theological differences."[9] Wurzburger went on to state that "Religion is neither politics nor business. In the spiritual sphere one cannot settle issues by making concessions. Total commitment is the very essence of a religious attitude. But what is needed is the ability to transcend institutional or denominational concerns in the quest for solutions that will enhance the welfare of the entire Jewish people."[10]

This transcendence was the basis for the community day school movement. From its inception, it had declared itself to be pluralistic, saying that its schools were committed to a set of principles which represented an ideological model for transideological Jewish education. They acknowledged the validity of all major streams of Jewish thought, and the incorporation of this principle into the curricula of community day schools. This acknowledgement implied that there were many possible options for the expression of Judaism. In addition, the group underscored the importance of showing appreciation and advocacy for the value concept of *Klal Yisrael* and the promotion of participation in Jewish community life.

Yet this characterization did not go unchallenged. The 1989 *Jewish Community Day School Network Newsletter* squarely confronted some of the existential issues the new network faced. In a provocative and thoughtful

---

7. Bulka, *Cataclysm*, 43.
8. Bulka, *Cataclysm*, 120.
9. Wurzburger, in Bulka, *Cataclysm*, 11.
10. Wurzburger, in Bulka, *Cataclysm*, 11.

article entitled "Crucial Challenges Face Community Day School Network," Allen Silver, head of the Jewish Day School of Seattle, directly addressed the issues of pluralism and transideology. He noted that the JCDSN was a fledgling young network in the early stages of defining "who we are and for what we stand." He urged caution in reference to the term "pluralism," noting that "I for one do not know what pluralism means and I'm not sure it's much clearer to most of my colleagues. I have found 'pluralism' to be a term that obscures rather than clarifies community issues. At the second RAVSAK Conference in Boston, Dr. Israel Schaffter suggested that we drop the term altogether. I agree. Let's call for a moratorium on 'pluralism' and force ourselves to define what we mean when we wish to use the term. We need to be equally careful in throwing about concepts such as respect, tolerance, validity, and transideology."

Silver also urged caution about the issue of diversity, worrying that too much openness and acceptance would lead to the meaningless conclusion that all religious paths are equally valid. "A number of Jewish texts make clear that Jews are to appreciate the existence of human diversity," he explained. "One of my favorite is the blessing recited when seeing an assembly of Jews: 'Blessed is He who discerns secrets, for the mind of each is different from that of the other, just as the face of each is different from that of the other.' While acknowledging the beauty of individual differences, Judaism does not elevate diversity to a sacred principle. The adage that 'there are 70 faces to Torah' (and only 70 faces) suggests that there is some limit to the number of ways we can look upon the world. In our RAVSAK discussions, I often feel that our lauding of pluralism contains the seeds of relativism, that anything goes in Jewish life. I'm sometimes reminded of a comment by Lionel Trilling that a person can have such an open mind his brains fall out."

As if anticipating the conflict that would arise decades later, Silver warned that the network needed to negotiate between "the twin pitfalls of absolutism and relativism." He stated firmly that "Community day schools should not seek to ascribe truth to all streams of Jewish thought" but rather "should work to foster a way of disagreeing that is informed by *derech eretz* and basic canons of civility. I don't mind if students at my school conclude that a particular approach to Jewish life is wrong. I am concerned how they relate to those who hold that opposing view. Will they be like Beit Hillel who openly taught and considered the views of Shammai or like Beit Shammai who closed themselves off from dialogue?"

Pluralism and Jewish Community Day Schools

Silver argued forcefully against the notion that knowledge, truth, and morality are not absolutes, but exist in relation to culture, society, and historical context. "Much effort at RAVSAK forums is devoted to outlining a community day school philosophy," he said. "Some have argued eloquently for the need to define a community ideology even while we recognize that our schools accept a range of practices. I sometimes wonder whether we're going at this the right way. We are inverting the classic Jewish concern to accommodate diverse ideas but exact a standard of common practice. We're all aware of the powerful line in the Talmud in which a voice from heaven responds to the debate between Beit Hillel and Beit Shammai and proclaims that 'these and these are the words of the living G-d.' What we tend to forget," Silver continued, "is the continuation of that *bat kol*: 'and the *halacha* is according to Hillel.' Ideological diversity can be encouraged but a community ultimately must share common practices for it to function as a community. Perhaps this classic Jewish model can help guide us in our goal-setting in individual schools and as a network." While acknowledging the value of transideological schools that expose students to a range of Jewish opinions, Silver stood firmly opposed to the creation of a generation of transideological students unable to develop or commit to a principled Jewish life.

In 1990, the Commission on Jewish Education in North America published a report entitled *A Time to Act* that opened starkly: "The Jewish community of North America is facing a crisis of major proportions. Large numbers of Jews have lost interest in Jewish values, ideals, and behavior, and there are many who no longer believe that Judaism has a role to play in their search for personal fulfillment and communality."[11] *A Time to Act* did not mince words: "In the face of such life-and-death issues [as Israel and Russian resettlement], the needs of education have seemed to be less urgent, less insistent, more diffused; a problem that could be dealt with at some point in the future when more pressing problems have been solved. This is an illusion. We may continue to live with emergencies indefinitely, but we can no longer postpone addressing the needs of Jewish education, lest we face an irreversible decline in the vitality of the Jewish people."[12]

Yet day schools received little attention in *A Time to Act*, being lumped in with "yeshivot, supplementary schools, synagogue-based programs of study and informal activities, community centers, programs at colleges and

---

11. Commission on Jewish Education, *A Time to Act*, 25.
12. Commission on Jewish Education, *A Time to Act*, 28.

universities, youth movements, summer camps, educational visits to Israel, early childhood programs, adult and family programs, retreat centers, and museums"[13] as educational providers. The one mention of day schools as unique entities was negative, saying only that "day schools have been increasing in number and size of student body; however, they still only reach twelve percent of the total Jewish student population. At present, the vast majority of Jewish parents choose not to enroll their children in a school environment they perceive as confining. Moreover, policy makers question the prospects of continued growth in light of the high cost of tuition, which is prohibitive even for many middle class families. At the same time, for many schools there is a severe shortage of qualified teachers and curricular materials."[14]

Despite its bold rhetoric, the solutions proposed by *A Time to Act* were bland. The core of the plan was "to infuse Jewish education with a new vitality by recruiting large numbers of talented and dedicated educators. These educators need to work in a congenial environment, sustained by a Jewish community that recognizes Jewish education as the most effective means for perpetuating Jewish identity and creating a commitment to Jewish values and behavior."[15] This kumbaya vision was to be accomplished through the achievement of five goals: 1. building a profession of Jewish education; 2. mobilizing community support; 3. establishing three to five lead communities; 4. developing a research capability; and 5. creating the Council for Initiatives in Jewish Education. Declaring its confidence that its "blueprint is realistic and feasible, and will indeed provide the foundation for a new era in Jewish education," the report nonetheless acknowledged that "an enormous investment of resources and energies will be required to bring this about."[16]

Filled with naïve optimism, the Commission on Jewish Education in North America asserted its conviction that "the will is there and the time to act is now."[17] Regrettably, the will was not there and the requisite "enormous investment of resources and energies"[18] did not materialize. The time to act passed without significant results. Five years later, a new commission, this

---

13. Commission on Jewish Education, *A Time to Act,* 32.
14. Commission on Jewish Education, *A Time to Act,* 34.
15. Commission on Jewish Education, *A Time to Act,* 17.
16. Commission on Jewish Education, *A Time to Act,* 18.
17. Commission on Jewish Education, *A Time to Act,* 74.
18. Commission on Jewish Education, *A Time to Act,* 18.

time the North American Commission on Jewish Identity and Continuity, issued yet another fifty-page report, titled "To Renew and Sanctify: A Call to Action." This report was significantly more positive about day schools, lauding them as "arguably the most impactful single weapon in our arsenal for educating Jewish children and youth." Unfortunately, the Council of Jewish Federations then decided not to heed the call or load the weapons in the arsenal by developing any national educational agenda or program.

Community day schools continued to make inroads in Jewish education but got little notice and even less respect. In the census of Jewish day schools in the United States published by the AVI CHAI Foundation in 2000, community day schools were given brief and unsympathetic treatment. The study's author, Marvin Schick, wrote that "Community day schools are diverse in their orientation and programs. Many are small institutions in a one-day-school community and others serve as the only alternative to the community's Orthodox day school. There is a loose association of these schools called the Jewish Community Day School Network or RAVSAK, although a considerable number get lost in the shuffle, living an independent and isolated existence. Community schools can have a Reform, Conservative, Reconstructionist or even modern Orthodox orientation."[19]

The community day school movement continued its growth, despite controversy about pluralism, theological differences, and a lack of recognition or support from the Jewish establishment. AVI CHAI's second census from 2003 to 2004 showed an overall increase in day school enrollment of eleven percent. But the number of community day schools had increased from seventy-five to ninety-five, while Schechter schools slipped from sixty-three to fifty-seven and Reform dropped by one. Schick acknowledged the community schools with some reluctance, saying "Among those who prefer non-Orthodox day school education, the recent stress has been on community or transdenominational schools. There are 20 more such institutions than there were five years previously, and they are responsible for the strong Community enrollment growth of 17%."[20]

Showing little admiration for community day schools, Schick gave even less credence to the "loose association" of RAVSAK, which he misspelled: "Because they are a varied lot, it's hard to pin down the Community day schools, although overwhelmingly and increasingly their Judaic curriculum and ambiance are weaker than what is found in Solomon Schechter

---

19. Schick, *Census* 2000, 7.
20. Schick, *Census* 2003–2004, 2.

schools. Many Community day schools are small institutions; at times they are the only day school in the community, while in some localities there may also be a small Orthodox School. A handful of schools that are now identified as Community were once designated as Orthodox, but with changes in the Jewish population, the leadership of these schools decided it is best to be transdenominational or a community school. There is a loose association of Community schools known as RavSak, an organization that has grown in its reach and professionalism, although its membership includes only about half of all Community day schools."[21]

In Schick's third census, published at the end of 2009, he finally acknowledged the meaningful existence of the "varied lot" of community day schools: "Community day schools continue to demonstrate growth, both in the number of schools — 98 in 2008–09 as compared to 75 in 1998–99 — and enrollment, which has grown by more than 40% over the past decade."[22]

Although he persisted in defining community day schools by what they were not (i.e., Conservative), Schick grudgingly gave some acknowledgement to RAVSAK (spelled correctly), which in his estimation rose from "loose" to "well-led." "Community Schools are the flip side of the Solomon Schechter picture. Most, but not all, of these schools are affiliated with RAVSAK, a well-led organization that has created a sense of affinity among schools that do not have a common denominational base. The transdenominational concept is much in favor these days among Federation and other Jewish philanthropic sources and also strikes a receptive chord among Jews who are nondenominational or, as they are now termed, post-denominational. Community schools are, inevitably, a varied lot. Among the nearly 100 in operation, a small number are close in Judaic ambiance to Modern Orthodox schools. As indicated, most are somewhat weaker in Judaics than the typical Solomon Schechter, although RAVSAK strives to strengthen member schools in this regard. How Community schools fare over the next decade will significantly determine the course of non-Orthodox day school education in the US. The current census dramatically indicates the growth and Community school enrollment. It was a 20% increase over the 2003 figure and, for the decade, the increase is precisely double that amount. Although some of this growth came from former Solomon Schechters now being identified as Community schools, the figure is impressive. Community schools now constitute far more than

---

21. Schick, *Census 2003–2004*, 13.
22. Schick, *Census 2008–2009*, 8.

half of all non-Orthodox day school enrollment and their share is likely to grow."[23]

Growth in the Jewish community day school movement was tied to what it represented. The twenty-first century model for community day schools was one in which pluralism was celebrated as a positive value that could be further expanded in the new technological sophistication, openness, and increasingly global worldview of the new millennium. The paradox of pluralism, as Michael Kay put it, is that "being well prepared to engage with diversity and difference in this world where community is defined by our differences not only strengthens individual identities but also strengthens our own connections to our community."[24]

The pluralistic spirit of the community day school movement resonated with many of the leaders of the twenty-first century non-Orthodox educational community. Rabbi Daniel Lehmann asked, "Is it not a fundamental tenet of our tradition that moral refinement is created out of the dialectic interplay of opposing perspectives? ... [Pluralism provides] an opportunity to create a new type of Jewish interchange that can shape a generation of Jews who understand the particularity of their own commitments in the context of the broader Jewish community."[25] Kay noted that "Pluralistic community schools constitute the only sector of non-Orthodox Jewish day school education that is experiencing growth, and thus the demand for comprehensive knowledge that can foster success in these schools is expanding rapidly. Fortunately, the level of enthusiasm in the field to persevere in the face of the evident challenges, to seek the benefits to individual and community that the enterprise of pluralism promises, and to continue to develop theoretical and practical approaches to enacting pluralism appears high."[26]

But pluralism as a label had become less than fully explanatory for many institutions. In the Autumn 2007 issue of *HaYidion*, RAVSAK's Executive Director, Marc Kramer, proposed a new description for community day schools. He suggested that a Jewish community day school is one "created in the image of the local community in which it is found, and that ... understands Jewish diversity as a strength and not a threat."[27] He

23. Schick, *Census 2008–2009*, 10–11.
24. Kay, "The Paradox," Para. 8.
25. Lehmann, "The promise," 2.
26. Kay, "Threefold Pluralism," Para. 22.
27. Kramer, "Thoughts," Para. 1.

distinguished between pluralism as an ideology "that suggests that divergent paths can and will be positively altered in the presence of others," and diversity, which is "an unbiased, non-hierarchical acknowledgement of the vast potential that will arise by welcoming and honoring the myriad expressions of what it means to be a Jew into one school."[28] He described the Jewish community day school as "an ingathering of hyphenated-Jews: Torah-observant-Jews, black-Jews, Jewishly-unaffiliated-Jews, Sephardic-Jews, intermarried-Jews, liberal-Jews, gay-Jews, working-class-Jews, cultural-Jews, single-parent-Jews, very-Yekkish-Jews, Jews-by-choice, synagogue-affiliated-Jews, Jews-who-need-more-than-one-hyphen-Jews, and certainly more."[29]

In the RAVSAK president's column in the same issue, Susan Weintrob wrote complementary words. "Diversity should do more than create populations with different races, although that is a worthy goal," Weintrob said. "Diversity of voices and perspectives in our schools helps us to craft educational philosophy, a framework for community and a plan for outreach. Yet we know that any change brings tensions and challenges each day. At RAVSAK schools, with no specific rabbinic authority, no political guidelines, and no imposed educational standards, a school may struggle in its creation and implementation of its own community values. Celebrating diversity should open the door to Jewish families, creating common ground for those in our community raising Jewish children." She continued, "While we may not welcome the tensions that diversity brings, they polish our values and aspirations, test our assumptions and stretch our notions of identity. These challenges help us confront whether we are comfortable dialoguing with those with whom we disagree, and help us to learn to respect those who may pray differently or eat with different standards. We should, with the right process and values, create a community with those whose families are structured differently and who may think or live differently."[30]

Weintrob explained the significant difference between RAVSAK schools and other day schools, "While many other schools have diverse populations, few encourage the dialogue among families, staff and students that we generate in RAVSAK schools." She noted, "We are used to exchanges of ideas. Once a Christian student of my husband asked me how we knew what the right way to read the Bible was. My answer was to show him a

---

28. Kramer, "Thoughts," Para. 2.
29. Kramer, "Thoughts," Para. 5.
30. Weintrob, "From the Desk," Para. 1.

Talmudic page. 'But which one of the rabbis' views is the truth?' he asked. I explained that all were considered holy. The study of many points of view is not only a commandment but a way of life. Diversity in our schools should create a living Talmud page."[31] The expansion of the definition of community beyond the limits of the term pluralism to include diversity of socio-economic background, gender identification, sexuality, color, and ethnicity, and the willingness to welcome all students and teachers and find ways to validate them within the school community, was an extremely meaningful step for the Jewish community day school network, further aligning it with modernity while at the same time further estranging it from other day school networks.

In opposition, Rabbi Shmuel Kaplan wrote a confrontational diatribe against pluralism and Jewish community day schools on the first day of 2013 under the title "Jewish Religious Pluralism Is a Destructive Idea." Kaplan stated that "the slogan of 'religious pluralism' has become a banner around which the American Jewish community has gathered and found common purpose. Pluralism — being accepting of and equating all ideologies and religious expressions — seems to be a wonderfully progressive idea in which all but the most 'bigoted' or 'narrow-minded' Jewish religious fanatics (read hareidi, Orthodox) can find common cause."[32] However, he went on to say that "The purpose of Jewish education is not just to produce educated Jews but to produce passionate Jews committed to the values and history of our people and our religion."[33] In Kaplan's view, a pluralistic school cannot do that. He gave the following example to prove his point: "Is *kashrut* an antiquated relic of pre-modern man that has no relevance to us today (the classic Reform ideology)? Is it an inspired religious practice, albeit one that needs to be modified and updated to fit our times (the Conservative ideology)? Or is it a Divine commandment that is immutable, including every detail of its Divinely inspired oral law (the Orthodox ideology)? If the answer is 'any of the above' then all of it is essentially meaningless. You can now repeat this same scenario for almost every important Jewish subject to be taught in a pluralistic Jewish school. Jewish education requires clarity of purpose, values and message. Anything less cannot produce the enduring results for the future that our people require."[34]

31. Weintrob, "From the Desk," Para. 1.
32. Kaplan, "Destructive," Para. 1.
33. Kaplan, "Destructive," Para. 5.
34. Kaplan, "Destructive," Para. 6.

Two Jews, Three Opinions

In Kaplan's view, "What we need is for each denomination to have its own schools. The Reform should teach that their view of Judaism is correct and teach why they think the Conservative and Orthodox philosophies are wrong. Let the Conservative and the Orthodox do the same thing: let them boldly state that 'we are right and they are wrong' and here is why. That is the kind of education that can succeed in producing committed and passionate Jews."[35] Having put Jews into self-contained mutually exclusive worlds, Kaplan noted that "the remarkable success of the Orthodox community in America—despite all the predictions and odds—should prove conclusively the validity of holding fast to one's values. It is time for the rest of the community to come to grips with this reality and abandon the easy foolhardy and naïve banner of pluralism that leads nowhere."[36]

Kaplan's views ran counter to those of many other commentators. Arie Hasit, writing in *Haaretz*, challenged the idea that Orthodox Judaism was the only true Judaism, even when "pluralistic Orthodox Jews are pluralistic in recognizing multiple truths, but orthodox in seeing one practice as the right way."[37] He noted that "the Mishna, the first law code of rabbinic Judaism, is replete with multiple opinions toward the same concept, and the Talmud has many unresolved debates in which the final *halacha* is not made clear. The schools of Rabbi Ishmael and Rabbi Akiva had completely different understandings of the biblical word 'ger,' stranger, and the laws they taught reflected those differences. It would indeed be difficult for someone to claim that one of those rabbis practiced authentic Judaism while the other simply created a compromised version that made Judaism more palatable."[38]

He concluded by saying, "To all those who can accept that Judaism is more complex than a singularly accepted set of practices, I'd like to emphasize that my brand of Judaism, Masorti (Conservative) Judaism, is not a watered-down version of some truer Judaism, but a valid interpretation of Judaism with its own merits. I believe the same is true of the other streams, but I will leave it to their adherents to proclaim their value. For my Judaism is rooted in Jewish law and in Jewish morals, in a Jewish decision-making progress and a Jewish sense of love for my fellow human beings and respect

---

35. Kaplan, "Destructive," Para. 9.
36. Kaplan, "Destructive," Para. 13.
37. Hasit, "In Defense," Para. 3.
38. Hasit, "In Defense," Para. 4.

for all humanity."³⁹ Those in the Reform movement expressed similar sentiments. "To be a Reform Jew in the twenty-first century is not as delimited as it was 50, 100, or 150 years ago," wrote Kate Judd in an article about the challenges of religious pluralism. "Some wear *kippot* and *tallitot*, some do not. Some keep kosher, some do not. Some worship mostly in Hebrew, some worship mostly in English. Even more important, affiliation with a movement does not have to imply the exclusion of other expressions of Judaism."⁴⁰

A nascent Pluralistic Judaism movement espoused many of these same sentiments, as explained by Rabbi Barbara Aiello, the first female rabbi in Italy. "This new movement is based on the Jewish concept of '*Tarbut HaMachloket*,' which, in Hebrew means 'freedom of thinking and speech,' and includes behaviors which help Jews of all backgrounds live successfully alongside those Jews with whom one might not agree."⁴¹ She noted that pluralistic Judaism is open and welcoming to Jews of all backgrounds, because it is non-denominational, unaffiliated, and does not distinguish between Jews by birth and Jews by choice. She further explained that "Pluralistic Judaism acknowledges that the word '*halakah*' is based in the Hebrew root, '*holech*,' which means 'to walk.' Thus *halakhah* is a changing phenomenon, implying that Jewish law moves forward and embraces new knowledge. Pluralistic Judaism is dedicated to achieving a balance between Jewish tradition and new ideas so that Judaism becomes and remains relevant to modern life. We subscribe to the joyful aspects of Jewish observance and we dedicate ourselves to maintaining warm relationships with each other and with the larger community."⁴²

While the precise definition and implications of pluralism proved elusive and subject to continual revisions and disquisitions, the Jewish community day school movement accepted pluralism at face value and bore down on the question of how to apply the tenets of pluralism, inclusion, and diversity in the classroom and school settings. In this endeavor, RAVSAK simply pushed ahead. "We promote academic excellence, maximal inclusion, Jewish diversity, and religious purposefulness," RAVSAK declared on its website, which was taken down when Prizmah was formed. "We believe that the future of the Jewish People is enshrined in *Klal Yisrael*—the notion

---

39. Hasit, "In Defense," Para. 6.
40. Judd, "Challenges," Para. 8.
41. Aiello, "Pluralistic," Para. 3.
42. Aiello, "Pluralistic," Para. 10.

of Jewish Peoplehood. RAVSAK is dedicated to empowering professionals to educate children and their families from across the spectrum of Jewish life."

As the self-defined international center for the advancement and support of pluralistic Jewish day school education, RAVSAK declared that its purpose was to strengthen and sustain "the Jewish life, leadership and learning of community day schools." Pluralism, it declared, "can signify everything from diversity in affiliation, tolerance, and representation to deep understanding of and engagement with conflicting Jewish perspectives. It is crucial for school leaders to understand and weigh different approaches to pluralism, to consider strategies and challenges of implementing pluralism, and to set policies and curriculum that align with the school's vision and values."

RAVSAK advocated for inclusion, saying that "diverse student bodies create an enriched educational environment for all, fostering compassion and understanding for peers who have a variety of physical, emotional, behavioral, or health challenges. Inclusive learning environments add intellectual, social, and spiritual benefits. These environments foster open learning spaces that encourage the sharing and exchanging of unique experiences and challenges, and work towards instilling the acceptance of all people regardless of their differences. At the same time, it defined Judaic studies as "the core of the Jewish day school experience, providing students with critical links to their past and giving them deeper context for their own experiences in the present."

But most importantly, RAVSAK provided multiple platforms and forums in which discussions of pluralism and its resonance could be held. A review of topics that appeared in the Winter 2009 issue of RAVSAK's journal *HaYidion* on the theme of pluralism gives an idea of the scope of these conversations: "Threefold Pluralism: A Strategy for Building 'Hybrid' School Community," "It Can't Be About Pluralism," "Tolerance: For a Minimalist Definition of Pluralism," 'Pluralism: The Demographic Reality," "Rival Versions of Pluralistic Jewish Education," "Israeli *Shlichim* in Pluralistic Schools," "Toward a Pluralistic Form of Peoplehood," "Can Pluralistic Schools Accommodate Everyone?," "The Influence of Pluralism on High School Students," "Transitioning to a New Model of Pluralism," "Teaching Pluralistically in a Reform Jewish Day School," "Pluralistic Day School Collaboration," "Fundraising in a Pluralistic Setting," "Pluralism in RAVSAK Schools," "Jewish Education in the Postmodern Era," "Spiritual Lessons in the Tensions of Halakhic Debate," "Pluralism in the Teaching of *Tanakh*," "How to Produce Pluralistic Jewish Educators," "Training Teachers for Pluralistic Day Schools," and "The Art of Pluralist Jewish Education."

The topic was not limited to this themed issue. *HaYidion*'s 2013 "Bold Ideas" issue included articles entitled "Hands-on, Inclusive Education: Building a New Future for Day Schools," "Beyond Denominations: Expanding Pluralism in Day Schools," "Cosmopolitan Jewish Education for the Jews Next *Dor*," and "A Community Day School for the Whole Community." The Autumn 2014 issue "Mission and Vision" included an article on "The Pluralistic Mission in Everyday Practice" as well as articles entitled "Pluralism: An Inquiry" and "Pluralism, Ethnos, Creativity and Israel."

Sessions at RAVSAK conferences were devoted to the theory and practice of pluralistic education in a community setting. In particular, Hebrew College President Rabbi Daniel Lehmann delivered the opening keynote at the 2014 RAVSAK/PARDeS Jewish Day School Leadership Conference in Los Angeles. A Jewish innovator who devoted his career to pluralistic Jewish education, Lehmann discussed "Beyond Continuity, Identity and Literacy: Making a More Compelling Case for Jewish Day Schools to 21st Century American Jews."

Enlarging the definition of pluralism well beyond the parameters set by the founders of the Jewish community day school network, he declared, "Jewish particularity should also be a catalyst for the development of universal ideals and global consciousness. We need to make a more cogent case that the particular values and pathways of Judaism can enrich the life of the individual in relationship to the global community and that through that particular we bring blessings to the universal: *Venivrchu becha kol mishpachot ha'adamah*, And through you, all families of the earth will be blessed."[43] In Lehmann's view, Jewish day schools had an enormous and challenging opportunity. He asked, "Can we envision our schools as communities of creativity, hubs of hybridity, centers of spirituality, places of particularism that open out to the universal and epicenters of ethical audacity?"[44]

Invited to respond to Lehmann's call in the Autumn 2014 issue of *HaYidion*, Shaul Magid wrote, "The challenges of post ethnic America require more than tinkering with an existing system; they require a complete reappraisal of the educational goals of identity formation. This is because

43. Lehmann, "Beyond Continuity," 16.
44. Lehmann, "Beyond Continuity," 16.

we live in an era where religion has ceased serving as the primary anchor of Jewish identity. Ethnicity, loosely defined, is now how many young American Jews identify as Jews. Religion serves more as a secondary, or tertiary, means of ethnic expression rather than a foundation of belief and practice upon which Jewish identity is forged," Magid said. "Yet today that ethnic anchor has been destabilized by numerous factors including the reality that the American Jewish community, like Americans more generally, are increasingly multi- or post-ethnic. Being 'ethnically Jewish' is now far more complex than it was even in the 1970s. And the acceptance of 'Jewishness' as an integral part of the American landscape, in culture, literature, film and politics, makes 'Jewishness' as something exclusive to Jews more complicated and nuanced. Ironically, Jewish success in America makes Jewish identity formation more, not less, difficult."[45]

Steven Lorch made an even stronger case for pluralism, arguing that "anyone who believes that his or her perspective captures the truth is both mistaken and arrogant. The best that human beings can do, in the face of profound unknowability, is to pool all of the imperfect perceptions of those who have carefully studied and pondered a phenomenon. The closest approximation of the truth is not the flash of brilliance of the greatest mind, but rather the gradual accretion of small insight upon small insight that comes from maintaining an openness to multiple perspectives. Pluralism, that is, an energetic and committed engagement with diverse ideas, understandings and perspectives, is an imperative because it offers the best hope of achieving true knowledge."[46]

"Judaism has always been diverse," writes Sylvia Barack Fishman, "but nothing compared to the varieties of the Jewishness that emerged as modernity transformed Western societies. Concepts of an organically evolving Jewish religious culture, the opportunity to examine that culture rationally and scientifically, and secular ideas and movements produced an unprecedented range of variations in how Jews defined their own Jewishness."[47] After thirty-six years, the community day school movement had come of age and had made diversity and pluralism its hallmarks. RAVSAK stood firmly in the forefront of day school education in its understanding of and commitment to Jewish education that was inclusive, pluralistic, and designed to foster religious purposefulness. True to its beginnings, RAVSAK repre-

---

45. Magid, "Pluralism, Ethos, Creativity," 28.
46. Lorch, "Pluralism: An Inquiry," 27.
47. Fishman, *The Way*, 209.

sented more than 130 schools that likewise sought to provide a pluralistic foundational Jewish education in a community setting. RAVSAK schools had dispensed with the particularism of Judaism in favor of its universalism, seeking to provide educational excellence for Jews seeking engagement with the larger society within the framework of meaningful Jewish lives.

4

The Rise of RAVSAK

In heaven there is truth; on earth there are truths.
RABBI LORD JONATHAN SACKS[1]

THE TWENTY-FIRST CENTURY OPENED with a spectacular announcement from RAVSAK Chair Karen Feller: "The Jewish Community Day School Network, one of the fastest growing Jewish educational associations in the North America, is at a critical turning point, and we need your help! After years of operating as a lay-lead, loosely organized group, we have recently made giant steps in professionalizing our work. Attending to the needs of over 70 schools, 200 administrators, 2,400 teachers and 17,000 students, we stand at the threshold and cutting edge of Jewish day school education and leadership."[2] She declared that if RAVSAK was to capture its most appropriate place on the national day school agenda, it needed to hire a full-time director and establish a national office in New York City.

Feller reported that a taskforce had met for an intensive session to set goals and develop objectives for the future of the organization. The task force had made it clear that funding was at the core of their planning. They had written a compelling case statement for giving and developed a modest

---

1. Sacks, *Dignity,* 64.
2. This and subsequent quotations and citations are from primary sources in possession of the author and archived at the American Jewish Archives, 3101 Clifton Ave., Cincinnati, OH 45220

The Rise of RAVSAK

three-year initial budget, which they planned to present at the January conference, asking the membership for feedback. Feller concluded with an impassioned plea: "We need your voice; we need commitment; and yes, we need to raise significant funds. In order to fulfill our mission, we also need each and every member of RAVSAK to see himself or herself as a partner in this incredible endeavor. Please come to the conference prepared to explore the potential that lies ahead. Remember that together we may be able to cultivate and influence the philanthropic generosity necessary to make this vision a reality."

RAVSAK had become the second largest Jewish school organization in North America. Marc Kramer was hired as executive director. He had been head of the Beit Rabban School in New York City and the Director of Judaic studies for the El Paso Hebrew Day School in Texas. He also had previously served as a consultant to RAVSAK. The RAVSAK office was moved to New York City and, in fact, was located in Kramer's apartment where space was at a premium. Key goals were to expand RAVSAK's membership to include all non-denominational Jewish day schools in North America, to offer more service consultation to schools, and to become a recognized presence in the constellation of Jewish educational organizations.

A cultural shift was simultaneously occurring in the Jewish community writ large. Federations, which had once rejected day school education as un-American, now proudly called their local day schools the "jewels in the crown" of their community achievements. By the end of 2003 the percentage of children in Jewish day schools was higher that it had ever been, and day schools were identified as the medium of hope for a North American Jewish future. Membership in RAVSAK grew from sixty to more than one hundred schools from 2000 to 2005, with much of the growth coming from schools opening in communities where a day school education had never previously been an option.

Community day schools overall were serving nearly 30,000 students, most from families that would not otherwise have opted for a Jewish day school education. Robin Feldman, who had previously worked with Kramer at the El Paso Hebrew Day School, was hired as RAVSAK's second full-time employee. Her title was director of membership and events, and she was put in charge of membership outreach, network communications, and planning the annual conference. She and Kramer worked together in his apartment, using makeshift desk space, sometimes a collapsible dining tray. Later, when Kramer's family grew, he moved to a larger apartment and

RAVSAK got its own room with a door. With the expansion of primary into secondary schools, Jewish high school membership in RAVSAK doubled. Talks began with the National American Association of Jewish High Schools (NAAJHS) about extending services to them, including hosting NAAJHS schools at the annual conference in 2005. Several previously unaffiliated schools joined RAVSAK, as did schools in Mexico and the United Kingdom. RAVSAK's annual Leadership Conference experienced significant growth. Fifty-six people attended the 2003 conference in Tucson; three times that number came for the 2005 conference in Irvine, California.

RAVSAK's programming was strong. Most notable was Project SuLaM: Study, Leadership and Mentoring (and also a play on the word *"sulam"* in Hebrew, which means "ladder.") Sponsored by the AVI CHAI Foundation and planned in partnership with the Brandeis University Summer School, the Florence Melton Adult Mini-School, and JSkyway, Project SuLaM was designed for heads of school who were established educational leaders but who lacked a meaningful Judaic studies background. It provided a cohort of heads of schools with an intensive year of Judaic studies, working with program staff, leading voices in Jewish studies, and expert Judaic mentors. Project SuLaM was devised to exert a transformative impact upon Jewish day schools. Premised upon a profound faith in the people who lead schools, SuLaM was created in the belief that great changes start from the top. Through close attention to its participants' learning and growth, SuLaM's goal was to cultivate the tools, skills, and dispositions in a generation of day school administrators that would allow them to take ownership of their schools' Jewish vision. Additionally, it forged a community of professionals who, through their school leadership, informal networking, alumni *Shabbatonim*, personal learning, and numerous other channels, continued to promote the values of the program and to strengthen their personal and professional bonds.

Another RAVSAK project, the Interschool *Tzedakah* Campaign, identified and coordinated common-cause *tzedakah* projects for member schools. These campaigns purchased an ambulance for the City of New York, supplied Magen David Adom with a mobile intensive care unit, planted more than 1,000 trees in Israel, stocked homeless shelters with several weeks' worth of non-perishable goods, and raised more than $40,000 toward renovating the New Orleans Jewish Day School after Hurricane Katrina. In conjunction with the Jewish Fund for Justice, RAVSAK also trained teachers from thirty member schools in the development and implementation of a social justice/*tzedakah* curriculum. In partnership with Facing History and Ourselves, RAVSAK arranged for middle and high school teachers of both general and Judaic studies to attend intensive training sessions on the teaching of the Holocaust. In the professional development arena, RAVSAK established a Head of School Network with peer-to-peer guidance available through a password-protected bulletin board and regularly scheduled conference calls. The network was used as a community of mutual support, as a launchpad for formal mentoring for novice school leaders, and as a forum for addressing questions of Jewish diversity.

In the service area, RAVSAK provided member schools with pro bono and reduced-cost graphic design services, technology support, and website hosting on its server. RAVSAK built seven school websites, designed four school logos and letterhead, and hosted more than half of small school websites. Some twenty member schools annually were assisted with telephone and on-site consultation services on a wide range of management and pedagogic issues, board retreats, Judaic curriculum reviews, and staff trainings. RAVSAK's executive director, Marc Kramer, provided unlimited telephone consultation to heads of schools and board presidents, often on confidential and critical issues or crisis management, frequently working late into the night to accommodate lay leader schedules and regional time differences. He also played a leading role in head of school searches.

RAVSAK undertook a number of research projects related to Jewish community day school management, Judaic policies and protocols, demographics, Israel education, and school finance. The findings of these research projects were distributed to member schools, prompting many to re-examine matters of Jewish culture (*kippot* and *kashrut* policies, multiple *minyanim*, for example) as well as management issues such as financial aid, severance, and board composition. RAVSAK developed a research protocol to generate detailed community portraits that were designed to help schools determine faculty compensation levels, better understand local Jewish community composition, and promote the strengthening of schools' Judaic programs. RAVSAK established working partnerships with other organizations dedicated to the advancement of Jewish day school education, including PEJE, NAIS, JESNA, DeLeT, HIAS, the Melton Center for Jewish Education and the denominational day school networks.

New student programs included Re/presenting the Jewish Past and the Jewish Court of All Time (JCAT). Re/Presenting the Jewish Past focused on improving how students encounter the Jewish past in their high school education and was run jointly by New York University's Steinhardt School of Human Development, Education and Culture and RAVSAK. Fully funded by the AVI CHAI foundation, the program partnered with schools to craft and implement a vision of Jewish history education that supported each school's mission and was both intellectually robust and personally meaningful to students. The Jewish Court of All Time allowed middle school students to explore contemporary issues through the perspective of an assigned historical figure, connecting and debating with peers via an online social platform with support from students and faculty from the University of Michigan, University of Cincinnati, Hebrew College, and the Davidson School at the Jewish Theological Seminary.

Marc Kramer was the right leader at the right time for RAVSAK. The self-defined "product of a Jewish intermarriage between a nominally Reform father and ritually-committed, deeply spiritual mother," he was raised in a Jewish environment "framed by the appositional notions of commitment and compromise."[3] Each member of his family was encouraged to forge a personal Jewish pathway with but two limitations: that it neither infringed upon the Jewish life of another nor prevented the family from celebrating together. Thus he learned "what it meant to simultaneously live within and beyond denominational norms."[4] In 2007, Kramer was awarded the prestigious Covenant Award, given to honor and celebrate those who have made an impact on Jewish life through innovative educational practices and models.

Kramer's impact and standing in the Jewish educational world and its environs was obvious from the words of those who nominated him. Lynn Raviv, a past president of RAVSAK, wrote, "Marc's transformational leadership has allowed RAVSAK to evolve from a loose affiliation of schools into the central address for community day school education. He has crafted a vision that ensures that children from across the spectrum of Jewish practice are able to flourish in rich, pluralistic settings. Marc has fashioned the organizational structure of RAVSAK to meet the diverse needs of member schools and to help these schools build capacity. Because of Marc, RAVSAK is able to offer its member schools the support and resources to meet the increased demands for excellence in Judaic and secular education. As a result, RAVSAK has become the fastest growing network of Jewish day schools

---

3. Covenant, *Award*, 1.
4. Covenant, *Award*, 1.

and high schools in North America."[5] Susan Weintrob, head of the Hannah Senesh Community Day School, wrote that Kramer "intuitively knows the direction and needs of the Jewish community in North America. Through RAVSAK, Marc has created a vision for education and leadership for the North American Jewish community."[6]

HaYidion, RAVSAK's erstwhile newsletter, was fast becoming a professional journal, appearing in 2005 in a new two-color magazine format with columns, articles, ads, photos, and glossy paper—a total redesign of its look. It was sent to 700 individuals and organizations, up from fewer than 300 in the past. Costs had increased to $2,500 per issue, and because ad revenue was only $1500, what had previously been a $300 profit per issue became a $1,000 expense. Because of the growing influence of the journal, however, these costs were covered as operational expenses, although sponsorships and increased ad revenue were sought.

RAVSAK conferences had become a force in the Jewish day school world. Where once attendees could fill the seats at a large table, annual RAVSAK conferences had become three-day meetings of concurrent sessions, attracting hundreds of participants and engaging leading educators and inspirational speakers for keynote addresses on current research and best practices. In 2006 there were 108 RAVSAK schools and the annual conference attracted 180 attendees. The following year, RAVSAK sponsored a joint conference with Pardes, the Reform day school network, and attendance was 225. At the RAVSAK annual meeting, there were glowing reports of new schools, new offices, new staff, new beginnings, new initiatives, and new challenges, while at the same time there was awareness of the need to address the emerging crisis in day school leadership of both heads of schools and boards.

As RAVSAK grew and its reach extended, it was becoming clear that dues and program fees were insufficient to sustain the organization. The executive committee, under Chair Bathea James, discussed ways for members to become comfortable raising funds for RAVSAK, including having executive committee members make their own financial commitments. "We need to support our own organization 100% before we ask others and then we need to reach out to others in our community who support Jewish education," James said. RAVSAK needed to engage with philanthropic partners who could help it plan for the future. A meeting was arranged with

---

5. Covenant, *Award*, 1.
6. Covenant, *Award*, 1.

executive committee members, selected heads of school, and people from the philanthropic world to dialogue in a thoughtful way about how RAVSAK was funded and staffed and where it fit in the larger Jewish educational community.

In August 2006, RAVSAK received a one-time grant from The AVI CHAI Foundation of up to $50,000 for operational expenses related to new office space—rent, furniture, technology—and to contribute to the salary of a new director of development. The intent was to enable Marc Kramer to devote more of his time to strategic planning and program development. The grant was given anonymously by the foundation and included the proviso that "AVI CHAI's receptivity to any future proposal for RAVSAK's organizational development will depend on our satisfaction with your development of a compelling vision, a viable operational model and a realistic development plan for the advancement of our mutual goals." The RAVSAK office finally moved out of the Kramer home in 2006 and began operating out of modest quarters at 120 West 97th Street in Manhattan.

The AVI CHAI Foundation's 2005 Annual Report contained the first public announcement that the Foundation was planning to sunset in 2020. "As we balance the desire to leave an enduring 'legacy' with an appropriate focus on today's needs," the report stated, "our Trustees and staff recognize the opportunity for AVI CHAI to leave behind us a corps of donors, advocates and leaders committed to continued improvement and support of the day school and camping fields writ large—people whose interest and commitment to Jewish education go beyond individual schools to encompass the overall reach and excellence of the field. While AVI CHAI has no plan to enter the fundraising business . . . we do hope that our experience over the past 20 years will enable us to both inspire and inform new philanthropists investing their own resources and energies into day schools and camping."[7] AVI CHAI's Executive Director for North America, Yossi Prager, described another result of the decision: "In the course of our strategic planning, the Trustees undertook a project-by-project assessment of the current portfolio. The review was meant to identify those projects that should be continued because they are sufficiently successful, cost effective, and close to the core of what AVI CHAI seeks to achieve. Projects that did not meet this standard, including some excellent programs that were not central to our current agenda areas, were marked for winding down."[8]

---

7. AVI CHAI, *Annual Report 2005*, 14.
8. AVI CHAI, *Annual Report 2005*, 14.

The Rise of RAVSAK

In 2007, Elliott Rabin was hired as RAVSAK's director of educational programs, tasked with creating and managing programs for teachers, students, and administrators designed to raise the level of Jewish education. Under his leadership, RAVSAK created Project ROPE: Roots of Philanthropy Education as well as Jewish art and Hebrew poetry contests. Rabin also oversaw the Moot Beit Din and JCAT, the Jewish Court of All Time. He also worked closely with Marc Kramer on Project SuLaM, including curating its educational content and later running its alumni programming. What Rabin was not hired to do was edit *HaYidion*. However, because of his magazine background, especially his years as an editor at *Harper's Magazine*, it was a natural fit and eventually became the main focus of his work. Under his editorship, *HaYidion* evolved into the premier journal in the field of Jewish education, with theme-based issues on matters of educational significance written by respected contributors. Its readership extended far beyond RAVSAK's schools to many other Jewish networks, organizations, and thought leaders both in North America and in Israel.

Another significant achievement in 2007 was the absorption of NAAJHS, the North American Association of Jewish High Schools, into RAVSAK. It was announced that a decision had been made "to bring the vision and programs of NAAJHS under the RAVSAK umbrella to create a vibrant new Jewish High School Network out of the merger. Building on the pioneering work of NAAJHS and the unprecedented success and growing infrastructure of RAVSAK, we will be able to expand the catalogue of programs and services offered to Jewish schools across North America. Much hard work and planning have gone into this union and it is with great joy that we now invite all high schools to join our new-and-improved network." All Jewish high schools regardless of affiliation were eligible for membership and schools that had been paying dues to both organizations now had only to pay RAVSAK dues. RAVSAK's incorporation of the Moot Beit Din, a mock trial competition for high school students, was another feather in its cap, as this highly successful program would undergo tremendous expansion and greater success in the new setting.

The same year, RAVSAK was selected as one of the fifty most creative and effective organizations in the country by 21/64, a non-profit consulting division of the Andrea and Charles Bronfman Philanthropies. More than 500 Jewish organizations had been nominated for this award. RAVSAK was profiled in *Slingshot '07-'08*, a publication designed for funders who support innovative Jewish life. The *Slingshot* profile stated that "What started as a peer group for a dozen heads of day schools is now a burgeoning network of more than 112 post denominational schools, representing 35,000 students across the United States, Canada and Mexico. RAVSAK produces a quarterly newsletter about trends in day schools, hosts an annual conference, provides consulting services to its members, and links schools so that one does not have to reinvent the wheel when another has recently tackled a particular organizational challenge. In an era when more and more people define their Jewish identities by their behaviors and not by a collective identity, RAVSAK is also unique in that it is necessarily post denominational, although some Reform and Conservative day schools seek out RAVSAK for the exemplary services it offers. RAVSAK represents 'innovation on a traditional model.' It is worth watching even for non-day school funders because RAVSAK claims that 70% of the children in its schools are from families with no other ties to the Jewish community. If that is the case, day schools have a unique opportunity not only to teach the children but also to engage the parents."[9]

In December 2007, the AVI CHAI Foundation made the welcome decision that it had added a new category to its philanthropic activities: strengthening institutions. Explaining that it desired that certain organizations, which embodied one or more of AVI CHAI's core purposes, continue their work beyond the period of AVI CHAI's life, it declared its intention to dedicate resources to strengthen these organizations' operational capacities. The Foundation awarded RAVSAK a $600,000 three-year grant to enable it to build the organizational infrastructure necessary to fulfill its mission of supporting and enhancing the Jewish character and content of community day schools. In a 2007 internal document entitled "Strengthening RAVSAK," AVI CHAI further elaborated that "the network of Community day schools includes the broadest range of commitments to our goals of Jewish literacy, religious purposefulness and peoplehood/ Israel (LRP). At one end of the spectrum are prep schools for Jewish (and occasionally self-defined non-Jewish) children, where Judaic learning and religious purposefulness are kept 'lite.' At the other end, are Jewishly-rich institutions that explicitly promote Jewish practice and a sense of responsibility to the State of Israel. Many of our current programs aim to persuade and teach this range of schools, through their leaders and their teachers, to strive to accomplish more Judaically. RAVSAK is already a programmatic partner for AVI CHAI, and we believe it has an even larger role to play in

---

9 *Slingshot*, Para. 1.

The Rise of RAVSAK

the creation of a sense of a movement to advance LRP. If these schools are to advance as a movement, there needs to be something propelling them to think together, learn from each other together, and find common Jewish purpose together. We think that that something can and should be RAVSAK, under the leadership of Dr. Marc Kramer."

AVI CHAI had prepared a cogent and clearly-stated analysis of RAVSAK's situation, declaring that Marc Kramer had accomplished much in his seven years at RAVSAK. "He has grown it from a network of under 70 schools to almost 120 schools. Recently, RAVSAK absorbed the North American Association for Jewish High Schools, which had been moribund, and it has additionally agreed to provide programming for the Reform day school network. Kramer is held in high esteem and is in high demand by the community day schools around the country. He promotes LRP with the same vigor as AVI CHAI. But while schools would like RAVSAK to provide them with a menu of Judaic services—help building meaningful Tefilah programs, help hiring Jewish studies personnel, help engaging high school students Jewishly, help with curricular development in Jewish subjects—RAVSAK for now is basically a two-professional show, Kramer and Dr. Elliot Rabin, with an annual budget of $90,000 (not including Project SuLaM)."

Anticipating these conclusions and recognizing its interest in enabling RAVSAK's growth, AVI CHAI engaged the National Executive Service Corps (NESC) to help Kramer develop a strategic plan for a more robust and financially sustainable organization. To no one's surprise, the NESC concluded that RAVSAK's key niche was in providing schools with Judaic support and that to fulfill that core niche, RAVSAK needed to be institutionally and financially stronger. One helpful outcome of the NESC process was Kramer's growing recognition that while he was the appropriate educational leader for RAVSAK, he did not have the fundraising or board-development skills that the organization needed in order to grow. AVI CHAI therefore proposed to build an institutional infrastructure around Kramer which would require funding to support the hiring and salary for three years of a COO, and funding and moral support to enable the COO and Kramer to build an effective lay board. They believed that their investment would communicate to the day school field and other funders AVI CHAI's belief that RAVSAK was a key institution necessary for the fulfillment of the future to which the foundation was committed.

AVI CHAI was well aware of the risks in building an institution around a single leader, but stated that, "in this case, the leader is known to and admired by many of our staff and his constituents in the field; the field has demonstrated its profound and ongoing need for the services he aims to provide; and his work is core to AVI CHAI's mission and for AVI CHAI's core audience." They were persuaded that the benefits outweighed the risks and stated their intent to provide "active involvement, to steward the efforts as stated above to mitigate the inherent risks." Specifically, AVI CHAI "would aim to ensure that the future COO would also follow up on NESC's initial scan of the field, to gain a deeper understanding of how the field relates to RAVSAK and what keeps the schools in the network. In addition, we would expect that collecting ongoing feedback on new and continuing initiatives would be part of the regular work of a strengthened RAVSAK."

In April 2008, Kramer signed a letter of agreement with the AVI CHAI Foundation spelling out the terms, timetables, and organizational structures necessary to accomplish the goals for which AVI CHAI was providing funding: development of a lay board, hiring of senior staff, and meeting fundraising benchmarks. It was made explicit that AVI CHAI senior staff intended to work closely with Kramer in the appointment both of the lay board and staff, going so far as the make the COO hire subject to their approval.

In making the grant, AVI CHAI wrote of its belief that "If RAVSAK becomes stronger and more stable institutionally, it will even more effectively propel schools to think together, learn from one another, and find common Jewish purpose together" and declared that, "For AVI CHAI, this grant represents a first experiment in using our resources to strengthen an institution, rather than achieve a programmatic goal. We hope that the experiment will be mutually productive and satisfying." Benchmarks for success included the hiring of a top flight COO, the seating of an energetic lay board, the development of strategic programmatic and financial plans with a clear mission, objectives realizable within reasonable timeframes, and success in attracting funding from new and sustainable sources.

In June 2008, the RAVSAK executive committee met to review the work of the year. Chair Ray Levi presented a report on the strategic planning process, which identified needs and alternatives with regard to board structure, noting that finance was tantamount to everything in a transition from program and service fees to funders. Under a proposed new model, trustees would make substantive financial commitments, would not convene, and would provide an income stream, not program dollars. The executive director would meet with trustees and develop intimate but individual relationships with them. The board of directors would be drawn from the lay leadership of schools and would be asked for a commitment of $10,000 per year for three years. They would convene twice a year and have working committees. The executive director would report to the board of directors. There would be three advisory panels for heads, Judaics and lay leadership. These advisory panels would be attended by staff, not the executive director, and would not be part of the governance structure. The RAVSAK staff would consist of the executive director; an assistant director of educational programs, a director of institutional advancement, and staff for high school programs, marketing, development, conference, technology, and membership. The staff structure allowed for an heir apparent in addition to meeting immediate needs. The executive committee was assured that this proposal was not funder driven and that AVI CHAI's funding of $200,000 per year for three years was not for a specific position or title.

Members of the executive committee were upset about the tremendous shift in the governance structure and raised many questions about the plan. Did AVI CHAI count as a trustee? How would all the constituent groups work together? What connected the advisory panels to the staff? What connections would exist between the executive director and the membership of RAVSAK? What would happen to the public voice, the public face of RAVSAK? Would the mission of RAVSAK change? Why were there no educators on the board of directors? Kramer responded that RAVSAK had a mission and a vision that trustees were asked to share and commit to support. He noted that funders felt a substantive disinterest in blended or mixed boards of lay and professional leaders, seeing them as lower functioning and less effective. He acknowledged that while the proposed model had shortcomings, it was one that was used in other settings, such as universities. He reminded the committee that members contributed less than ten percent of RAVSAK's budget and said that the role of the executive director as the voice of RAVSAK needed to be more clearly stated as attending to the organization's bold vision.

Further discussion addressed the issue of how the constituencies that RAVSAK represented would be served by the new model. There was disquiet about having a board that set policy and direction without having professional educators as members. There was apprehension about what would get lost in the dramatic reorganization, the speed of the changes, and a deep fear that the nurturing aspects of RAVSAK would disappear. Members expressed the belief that RAVSAK couldn't just sell out to money; that it was a service organization with membership, distinguishing it from many other nonprofits, and that the loss of the executive director as the voice of RAVSAK was significant. They repeatedly emphasized the need for sophisticated educators on the board to represent the perspectives of the schools.

Ultimately, however, the consensus of the executive committee was that RAVSAK could not stay where it was, that it needed to do something or else go back to where it used to be. The members felt that they needed to listen to the executive director, while being sure that nothing happened that would cause RAVSAK to lose the status it had at that point in time. They reasserted the tenet that RAVSAK served the needs of educators and that those relationships were sacrosanct. Kramer responded that this was evolution, not revolution, and that he believed it to be critical that the organization have new leadership. He stated that the job of executive director needed to be defined and not as "everything to everyone." Blending the board to include professionals was not what donors wanted; they said it doesn't work, he explained, but conceded that, in the end, the decision was up to the executive committee. "We have to either scale up or scale back," he concluded. "We do not have the resources we need. We 'non-function' as a board. Asking heads of schools to take governance roles hasn't worked. This is not a leap but a process. We need to look at what the industry needs and wants and what a national organization needs to function."

Ray Levi concluded the session by saying that all agreed that that RAVSAK's governance was not functioning effectively and needed to be changed. He stressed that the main concern in the formation of a new governance structure was the maintenance of the educators' voices. Kramer assured the executive committee that he had heard their concerns and would develop a realistic timetable, but he stressed, "We can't be here a year from now having done nothing."

5

RAVSAK under New Governance—2010–2016

RAVSAK will transform Jewish life in North America and beyond by strengthening community day schools, encouraging religious purposefulness, and fostering authentic Jewish pluralism.[1]

THE YEAR 2010 MARKED a watershed for RAVSAK. The conference attracted more than 500 attendees and was the first joint conference sponsored by the RAVSAK, Yeshiva University, and the Pardes and Schechter networks. RAVSAK's ten-year report highlighted 120 member schools and declared that the growth in RAVSAK reflected the change and maturation of the North American Jewish community. RAVSAK proudly proclaimed itself the fastest growing network of Jewish day schools in North America. Its mission statement declared that in attending to the leadership and management needs of more than 120 schools serving nearly 30,000 students, it stood at the cutting edge of Jewish day school education and leadership.

The RAVSAK membership was asked to approve a major restructuring of the organization's governance model at the conference. A letter sent to member schools' leaders explained that RAVSAK had grown in numbers and range of services it provided for a significantly more sophisticated Jewish day school world. As the programming expanded and the professional staff grew, the leadership needs of the organization changed. When the

1. RAVSAK, *Our Client*, 4.

primary functions of the organization were planning a small conference and communicating through a newsletter, its financial needs were met by dues and its governance was in the hands of a committee of day school professionals. Both of those modalities had been outgrown.

"For the last several years," the letter stated, "we have engaged in a strategic planning process, in consultation with some of our major funders, and have explored governance models that will match our role as a major voice in Jewish day school education. We have known for a long time that our interests would be better served through the involvement of influential lay leaders who can provide and attract financial support to RAVSAK, so that we can offer the guidance and support to our network of schools that is both needed and valued by our membership." After extensive discussion, the executive committee voted to recommend a change in the governance of RAVSAK, to a transitional board of four to six lay leaders who would each contribute $10,000 or more; one to two professional representatives who would each contribute $1,000 and the executive director. This Board would then work to build a larger Board which would work to assure that RAVSAK had the financial resources to realize its mission and vision.

At what would prove to be its last annual meeting, the membership voted to create a new national board composed of philanthropic lay leaders and two professionals. In a clear response to the concerns of the executive committee, it was stipulated that the two professional members of the board of directors would be current or retired heads of RAVSAK schools. The board's charge was to refine and advance RAVSAK's vision on a global level. Arnee Winshall was named founding chair. Winshall had been the founding chair of Boston's Jewish Community Day School and a member of the boards of The Harold Grinspoon Foundation and the JCC of Greater Boston. She also had served on the executive committee of JESNA, as the lay chair of the Lippman Kanfer Institute, and on the board of the Foundation for Jewish Camp as well as being the founding chair of Hebrew at the Center, an entity dedicated to advancing Hebrew teaching and learning.

New mission and vision statements were approved, replacing ones drafted years before. RAVSAK's new mission was "to strengthen and sustain the life, leadership and learning of Jewish community day schools, ensuring a vibrant Jewish future." And the vision underpinning this mission was "a future where life in North America and beyond was enriched and elevated by generations of Jewish day school graduates who are Jewishly literate, proficient in Hebrew, profoundly connected to Israel, and actively engaged as the energizing nucleus of the Jewish community."

RAVSAK's values were detailed, with *Klal Yisrael* taking pride of place:

Klal Yisrael	The unity of the Jewish People
Talmud Torah	A commitment to life-long Jewish learning
Derech Eretz	The promotion of civil discourse
Tzelem Elokim	The importance of the individual, each created in the Divine Image
Tzionut	The centrality of Israel, Zionism, and the Hebrew language
Gemilut Chasadim	A commitment to teaching acts of righteousness
Iyun Tefilah	The promotion of religious purposefulness and the worthiness of prayer

New by-laws emphasized RAVSAK's commitment to pluralism, defining it as "the international center for the advancement and support of pluralistic Jewish day school education." Proudly proclaiming that "We promote academic excellence, maximal inclusion, Jewish diversity and religious purposefulness," RAVSAK declared that "We believe that the future of the Jewish People is enshrined in *Klal Yisrael*, the notion of Jewish peoplehood. RAVSAK is dedicated to empowering professionals to educate children and their families from across the spectrum of Jewish life."

The goals of RAVSAK were to:

- Enrich professional and lay leadership through programs and conferences that build position knowledge, develop leadership and managerial skills, heighten positive disposition, encourage tenure, and strengthen commitment to Jewish diversity;
- Develop protocol and policy best practice modules that ensure meaningful pluralism and equal the highest standards of leading independent schools;
- Promote religious purposefulness, a commitment to life-long learning, and the centrality of Israel—the land and its people, across time and today in our schools;

- Expand networking capacities within and across administrative positions to promote peer learning, reduce professional isolation, and foster a culture of mutual support;
- Facilitate student programming at the high school levels which provide opportunities for collective learning, tzedakah, and spiritual growth.

Addressing the assembled professionals and lay leaders of community day schools, the new Board chair Arnee Winshall listed the reasons she had agreed to head the new board. She highlighted the degree to which RAVSAK had realized its potential and its commitment to excellence as exemplified by the conference, Project SuLAM, the Moot Beit Din, and *HaYidion*, which she saw as the premier publication for day schools, as exemplified by the most recent issue which lead the thinking on intentional pluralism. Winshall emphasized that RAVSAK was an organization created of, by, and for its constituency, which recruited support to provide schools and school leadership with programs that sustained their success and which the schools themselves identified as critical. Distinguishing RAVSAK from other organizations whose agenda was set by donors, Winshall said, RAVSAK's agenda was set by its constituents. Donors supported the successful realization of that agenda.

Following the 2010 annual meeting, Sarah Kass from the AVI CHAI Foundation facilitated a meeting of the new RAVSAK board of directors: lay members Arnee Winshall, Lesley Zafran, and Paul Levitch, and professional members Bruce Powell and Barbara Davis. Zafran was the president of the board of Donna Klein Jewish Academy in Boca Raton, Florida, and chair of its Jewish Day Schools for the 21st Century program. She sat on the administrative leadership team for the creation of strategic plans both for the school and the board of trustees. Paul Levitch was president of Levitch Associates in Louisville, Kentucky. He had served on the boards of non-profits at the national and local levels including the Interdisciplinary Early Childhood Education (IECE) in Kentucky. He had experience in all the major aspects of board work, such as strategic planning, fundraising, and evaluating grant proposals. Bruce Powell was head of school at New Community Jewish High School in West Hills, California, and Barbara Davis was head of school at the Syracuse Hebrew Day School in Central New York. Although they were not representing particular constituencies other than school professionals, Powell was from a large school on the west coast

RAVSAK under New Governance—2010-2016

and Davis from a small school on the east coast, thereby achieving a semblance of balance of gender, school size, and geography.

Kass opened the meeting by saying that she felt that the transition was outstanding, that people felt power at being on the verge of something new, and that the conference was a testament to that power. There was a sense that RAVSAK started as being "not something," and has become the center, "the basis from which the future will emerge." "Post-denominationalism is where people are," she declared. Board members also shared their impressions. Zafran felt a sense of warmth and kindness, but felt the burden of the real work that had to happen beyond the words. Powell said that Marc Kramer was the only one who could have pulled off the leadership conference, with all the people in the same room. Levitch was taken by the lack of confusion at the transition; he had expected more challenges. Davis noted that the three-year process had resulted in buy-in and that people wanted to preserve what was great from the past while growing into a new future. Winshall remarked that young leadership was needed at the Board table, to challenge the board and to push it not to be complacent. Marc Kramer took note of two major accomplishments: getting a board and putting everyone under one roof. But he was struck by the number of things RAVSAK was asked to do that it could not, such as being a technology leader and assuring the survival of marginal schools. He wanted to focus on the big picture: RAVSAK as the central agency for progressive schools, the central address for all non-Orthodox day schools.

Kass then suggested that the board focus on where it should be two years hence in four key areas: trustees, executive support, development and marketing, and finance. The list of needs, goals, and ideas suggested by the group was lengthy: recruit seven additional lay Board members, three of whom are in their 30s and younger, who are people of substance and vision; create a culture of endowment, the only sustainable model; clarify the boundaries of what RAVSAK could do as an organization, avoiding hubris, and focusing on what RAVSAK does better than anyone else; examine, clarify, and simplify the mission and vision; develop strategic and financial plans; assure a broad base of directorship in terms of age, geographical diversity, and technological savvy; develop systems for board education, evaluation, and vetting new members; write a job description and contract for executive director; set standards and timelines for evaluation, and plan for succession; brand RAVSAK as an organization; develop a shared language; produce customizable materials for schools; create a steadier income stream for operations; develop an endowment fund; create a budget reflective of priorities and a five-year plan; write a story that tells itself; create an advisory "major support" committee; distinguish RAVSAK from PEJE and Lookstein; provide adequate compensation for the executive director; become a "board of choice" on which people want to serve; clarify roles of board and staff members; develop protocols, systems, and rules; raise core dollars; write investment protocols and policies; do a financial autopsy; obtain directors and officers insurance.

The ideas and suggestions were consolidated and converted into goals for the board committees and assigned to each board member. The board agreed to have weekly, focused one-hour conference calls, sometimes with a facilitator. The intent was to have clear inputs, clear processes, outputs, and outcomes.

Soon there were new faces around the RAVSAK board table. Uri Benhamron and Rebekah Farber became members in 2010. Benhamron, a native of Venezuela, was a principal at ISRAEL G-Tek, a Miami-based private equity fund investing in green technology companies. He served on the board of governors of the Hillel Community Day School in North Miami Beach and on the American Jewish Committee where he was chair of the Consular Corps Committee of the Latin American Task Force. A leader in her home community of Los Angeles, Farber brought energy, experience, and commitment to her position. She and her husband, Howard, were co-founders of the New Community Jewish High School in West Hills, California, and she had served on many philanthropic boards. Idana Goldberg, a consultant who had worked with the Jewish Funders Network after getting her doctorate in history, was hired as RAVSAK's associate executive director with a portfolio that emphasized taking RAVSAK to the next organizational level. Goldberg started work on July 1, 2010, believing that RAVSAK was at a prime moment to grow. Kramer told her that he could see RAVSAK consolidating all the non-Orthodox day school networks and growing as the center for non-Orthodox day school education.

The conference theme in 2010 had been "Thriving in a New Reality" and addressed twenty-first century challenges including economic uncertainties, government funding, demographic changes, and teacher retention. The conference also examined the promise of technology, Jewish service learning, and the use of social media to build educational communities. The gathering of nearly 600 educators and lay leaders was a breakthrough in exhibiting common purpose among Jewish religious streams. Marc

Kramer extolled the cooperation among Reform, Conservative, Orthodox, and community day schools as a bright new light for *Klal Yisrael*, proving that working across ideologies was possible.

The 2011 conference theme was "The High Performance, High-Tech Jewish Day School of the Very Near Future," designed to underscore how Jewish educational professionals were transforming their individual institutions —and the day school movement itself—into inclusive venues of educational quality and value utilizing proven, effective, and emerging approaches. Nearly 70 workshops focused on issues, ideas, challenges, and opportunities facing Jewish educational leaders, including the promises and pitfalls of Israel education, new technologies, philanthropic support, and education for students with special needs. Attendance at the 2011 conference was up by about twenty percent from the previous year, an increase attributed to the dynamic changes taking place within Jewish day schools and the conference as a venue for educators across practices to share approaches and learn together.

Paul Levitch stepped off the board and four new members joined in 2011: Lisa Breslau, Matt Heilicher, Stacey Fisher, and Joseph Steiner. Breslau was president of the Shalom School, which had been a member of RAVSAK since its founding. Heilicher was board chair at the Heilicher Minneapolis Jewish Day School. Stacey Fischer was past chair of the Rockwern Academy in Cincinnati, Ohio. "Joey" Steiner's career in volunteer Jewish community service revolved largely around Jewish education as a member of the board of Bialik Hebrew Day School, which he had served as president, and a member of the board of Paul Penna Downtown Jewish Day School. Bruce Powell left the RAVSAK board in 2012 to concentrate on fundraising for the New Jewish High School and was replaced by Zipora Schorr, director of education and head of school at Beth Tfiloh Dahan in Baltimore, Maryland.

In response to the need for board expansion and philanthropic development to support the growing organization, a five-year business plan entitled "Strengthening the Field" was drawn up. The outgrowth of extensive research, the plan prioritized areas of focus and identified needed resources for the period from 2012 to 2017, including staffing and finances. Four strategic priorities were identified: 1. connect school professionals and lay leaders with their peers in other community day schools and enhance their ability to learn from each other; 2. promote the benefits of community day schools, represent community day school interests, and equip schools to be advocates for themselves; 3. strengthen the Jewish literacy and leadership of community day school professionals and lay leaders, which would enhance their effectiveness in delivering educational value; and 4. provide a focused portfolio of direct programs for students that enriches their Jewish literacy and leadership.

The plan outlined a number of initiatives in each of these areas, including the expansion of existing programs and services and the creation of new ones. Although it did not describe a direct role for RAVSAK in devising strategies for schools to achieve fiscal health, it did address the long-term financial health of schools in three ways: 1. strengthening the Jewish educational excellence of schools through professional development, teacher pedagogy and enhanced subject-content areas, enhancing schools' ability to demonstrate their value proposition and elevate their position within their distinct markets; 2. marshaling resources and data from the national field, to support each school's opportunity to make its case and advocate for itself with families and local funders; 3. serving as the national representative of the Jewish community day school movement, elevating the national conversation and enriching the discourse around Jewish community day schools thereby encouraging greater philanthropic investment on a national level.

The business plan had a hefty price tag. It projected that RAVSAK's budget would grow from $2.0 million in fiscal year 2012 to $3.6 million in fiscal year 2016. Revenue growth was expected from a mix of sources, including membership fees, fees for service, and grants from individual donors and funding from philanthropic partners. In addition to an ideal scenario for RAVSAK's growth, the plan provided two additional scenarios to reflect how RAVSAK and its work would unfold in the event that actual revenues did not match expectations.

The plan made clear that RAVSAK could not go it alone; it needed substantial philanthropic support to meet its fiscal goals. The report put it plainly: "Having looked carefully at a range of economic alternatives, we have concluded that the realization of this plan will be possible only with the support of philanthropic partners—partners who seek to participate in strengthening the Jewish life, learning and leadership of schools by empowering RAVSAK to act as their agent for growth and change. Just as we at RAVSAK are inspired to take on the charge of strengthening our schools, we hope others will hear this call and join us in our work."

The business plan called for ambitious development benchmarks based on an optimistic scenario. Annual campaign gifts were projected to increase from $57,000 in in fiscal year 2013 to $84,700 in fiscal year 2015. Board giving was to increase from $125,400 to $165,400. Trustee level gifts were to increase from $50,000 to $200,000 and National Giving Society giving was to grow from $80,000 to $220,000.

There were major obstacles to achieving success at the called-for levels. Lesley Zafran could not continue to chair the development committee because it conflicted with her development work at Donna Klein Jewish Academy. The lack of a development director seriously impeded progress because neither board nor staff members had experience or expertise in fundraising for a national (as opposed to a local) organization. Nothing previously tried had been tied to a unified plan. The board itself still had a disconnect about what it was meant to do. Board members knew they were supposed to raise money for RAVSAK but did not feel they had a comprehensive and strategic plan for doing so. Development had become a key part of RAVSAK's work and a guiding hand was needed. The board agreed to draft a development plan and calendar for itself, with specific goals and assignments, of which it could take ownership, so that it was proactive rather than reactive to fundraising needs.

RAVSAK's success on the programmatic level, however, continued unabated. The Head of School Professional Excellence Project (HOSPEP) paired experienced heads of school with new heads in highly successful mentorships. RAVSAK *Reshet* (network) centers were created to focus on topics of interest to a variety of constituents, utilizing digital communications to forge meaningful connections among geographically diverse communities. Individuals working in job-alike groups (heads of school, board members, early childhood educators, Judaic studies directors) shared questions and concerns, successes and other experiences, with one another. The *reshetot* (networks) were busy with conversations that offered a fascinating window into the realities of day school operations. Questions were raised about hours on task in Jewish studies; how to measure student achievement in Hebrew; how to estimate construction costs for building renovations; how to deal with transgender students; how to make an Israel trip happen when money is tight and parents are willing to wait for a free Birthright trip; how to negotiate a new contract; and much more. There was also "spin off" activity such as off-line conversations, webinars and data collection. RAVSAK consulting and support services were in high demand and *HaYidion* saw record readership for themed issues on such highly relevant topics as marketing, technology, diversity, religious purposefulness, pluralism, special needs, strengthening community, nurturing faith and board leadership.

But Jewish education still faced many challenges. The field had gotten crowded. Many organizations wanted to be national players. There were new organizations such as the Jewish Futures Network and Project Leadership and large foundations had begun to run their own programming amidst a growing world of small organizations. Collaboration was being replaced by competition as many organizations sought to serve the entire field instead of a segment of it. RAVSAK was still in a position of strength, with new hires and programming, and a reserve account, but the fiscal future was uncertain.

In 2013, the RAVSAK board's founding chair, Arnee Winshall, turned over the reins of RAVSAK to Rebekah Farber. In her final column, for the "Bold Ideas" themed issue of *HaYidion*, she reflected on her tenure:

- *What was bold was the creation of community day schools and then the step that was taken over 30 years ago to create a network of these schools.*

- *What was bold was outreach to families beyond the orthodox community to commit to serious and joyous full-time Jewish schooling.*

- *What was bold (and wise) was to recruit Dr. Marc Kramer to grow and lead this organization.*

- *What was bold were the steps the Executive Committee took in 2008 to transition to an international board largely populated and guided by distinguished lay leaders committed to Jewish day school education.*

- *What was bold was for RAVSAK to undertake to invite and bring together all the day school organizations to provide a forum for growing and learning together resulting in the North American Jewish Day School Conference.*

- *What was bold was for the first Board Members to undertake the responsibility and dedicate their time, wisdom and resources to take RAVSAK to the next level.*

- *What was bold was for RAVSAK, with the AVI CHAI Foundation's encouragement, guidance and support, to undertake a thorough assessment and multi-year plan to guide the organization's and the field's growth.*

RAVSAK under New Governance—2010-2016

- *And what is bold is the undertaking of an ambitious effort to expand the scope of RAVSAK's work and its resources to ensure that it continues both to serve the field and to push the boundaries of the field.*
- *What was and continues to be bold is RAVSAK's unyielding commitment to excellence and responsiveness, which ensures its provision of field-wide and personalized attention enabling all our schools to become the best version of themselves."*[2]

In 2013, Shira Brown became RAVSAK's newest board member. Chief of emergency medicine for three hospitals in the Niagara Health System in Ontario, Canada, Brown was chair of philanthropy for the Kadimah School of Buffalo, New York. The majority of the RAVSAK board's time was spent on development issues and on the increasingly difficult challenge of raising funds to meet the specifications of the business plan. There were several staff hires who worked with limited success and insufficient tenure in fundraising. Despite the fact that the board had grown and that its members contributed generously to the organization, the financial situation did not improve because RAVSAK's expenses had grown significantly. Conversations at the lay board's meetings began to resemble those of the old executive committee, with constant reminders of the inadequacy of the fundraising achievement and the inability to sustain the organization without greater philanthropic support.

Farber and Kramer gave an update on the AVI CHAI Foundation Capacity Building Grant, saying that they had had lengthy conversations with AVI CHAI's leadership about RAVSAK's relationship with the foundation. Benchmarks were set, although, in RAVSAK leaderships view, the timelines were too ambitious. AVI CHAI expressed concern that RAVSAK had not met one of its most critical benchmarks, the growth of the board of directors, upon which the future of the organization depended. Farber emphasized that RAVSAK needed to develop relationships with other funders. "Our relationship with AVI CHAI is like a parent and child," she stated. "There is a high level of angst."

---

2. Winshall, "From the Desk," Para. 2.

6

The Demise of RAVSAK

Judaism has never been monolithic. There have always been varieties of Judaism. The more conservative Sadducees and the more progressive Pharisees represent only one of many past conflicts. We affirm the diversity of our tradition.

RABBI JOHN D. RAYNER[1]

IN 2014 RAVSAK MOVED from its cramped offices on West 97th Street to much larger quarters at 254 West 54th Street to accommodate its growing staff and programming. Architect Cassandra Gottleib joined the board. She had been a volunteer leader in the Jewish community for more than thirty years and had served as president of the board of trustees of Beth Tfiloh Dahan Community Day School. She also served as the national chair of JESNA, the Jewish Education Service of North America, the Jewish federation system's educational coordinating, planning, and development agency.

At the beginning of 2014, the RAVSAK board received a request from Marc Kramer to transition from full-time to part-time work. He wrote that he was making this change for family and personal reasons, stating that while he remained deeply committed to RAVSAK and its unique mission, he also believed that the organization was ready for a new executive. The board was willing to grant this request, recognizing Kramer's extraordinary

---

1 Rayner, *Affirmations*, 8.

The Demise of RAVSAK

work on behalf of the organization and because his workload had become too heavy. Board members had been concerned for some time that RAVSAK was a one-man operation and that the name RAVSAK was virtually synonymous with Marc Kramer. Neither the board nor Kramer felt that this was good, and although Kramer had made it clear from the time he hired Idana Goldberg that he considered her "an heir and a spare," the board felt that the time had come to hire a chief executive officer. To reassure the RAVSAK membership and the field that this in no way represented a demotion of Kramer and was, in fact, in response to his own request, the board drafted a statement explaining that organizational growth necessitated a reformulation of RAVSAK's operational structure to include a senior professional who would champion its national fundraising efforts, enhance organizational leadership and nurture inter-organizational relations. Marc Kramer would focus his efforts and expertise on fulfilling the programmatic mission of RAVSAK, particularly professional development, networking, student programming, and direct school services.

But three months later, Kramer modified his request, noting that proposed changes to the national educational landscape were such that a leadership transition at RAVSAK would neither be simple nor accomplish the stated goal of strengthening the organization. He explained that because the Jim Joseph and AVI CHAI Foundations believed that the current configuration of intermediary organizations was unsustainable, RAVSAK would soon find itself engaged in conversations about streamlining the field. This would, he thought, inevitably result in some degree of consolidation and possibly a full-scale merger of RAVSAK with PEJE, the Schechter network, Yeshiva University's School Partnership, and PARDES. He further warned that AVI CHAI had signaled that failure to meet its capacity grant benchmarks would result in the reduction or termination of its support for RAVSAK.

The board and staff then made a decision that was supported by its leadership and membership but not well-received by funders and others. Instead of participating in a joint North American Jewish Day School conference, RAVSAK held its own conference in Los Angeles in conjunction with Pardes, as it had years before. Many RAVSAK member schools had become disenchanted with the larger conferences, which they felt diluted the collegiality and comradery that community school heads valued so highly, and restricted conversations about such topics as gender inclusiveness, equality and fluidity, interfaith families, and *Klal Yisrael* that were unique to community schools. With a less cumbersome structure, RAVSAK was able to plan a more flexible and innovative conference. It was organized around Deep Dives, sometimes in partnership with other groups: Small Schools and a Sustainable Future (in cooperation with PEJE); New Paradigms for Israel Education (in partnership with the Shalom Hartman Institute of North America); Special Needs and the Diverse Classroom; Design Thinking and Adaptive Leadership (in partnership with Upstart Bay); Tefillah: New Paradigms (in partnership with Pardes Institute of Jewish Studies) and Effective Technology, Effective Education (in partnership with The DigitalJLearning Network of The Jewish Education Project).

RAVSAK's relationship with The AVI CHAI Foundation, its major philanthropic partner, was growing sour. Immediately upon the close of a successful conference in Los Angeles, Idana Goldberg reported to the board that, in the first year of the strategic plan, RAVSAK had failed to meet its benchmarks and now needed to determine how to reimagine them in line with actual achievement. An extended first year of eighteen months with a second year ending in December 2014 was created to allow for the completion of the Israel Initiative and *T'fillah* projects. AVI CHAI did not want to release its funding without completion of the goals. RAVSAK tried to reassure them that it was contributing tremendously to the field even though it had not done the two things they expected. AVI CHAI countered that RAVSAK had done nothing new and that they paid for new initiatives to invent the field. They were not happy that RAVSAK held a conference by itself instead of continuing the conference partnership of the previous three years. They wanted to unite the field. Discussion centered on the politics of the situation. It was acknowledged that RAVSAK needed AVI CHAI's funding or it would be bankrupt. It was emphasized that at the end of the day, RAVSAK had to follow through with its programmatic obligations.

The board discussed RAVSAK's relationships with other organizations in the field. RAVSAK believed that it had developed a strategic alliance with the Reform day school network and had crafted a statement to announce this natural alliance and easy confluence. The Pardes network consisted of thirteen schools, 5,000 students, and a governing committee of eight executive plus nine at-large members; they were an affiliate of the Union for Reform Judaism. Pardes was very involved with their movement's synagogues and wanted to maintain a relationship with Reform students in RAVSAK schools. They had rabbinic interns who might serve RAVSAK and they wanted to be able to advocate for their children to attend a day school. It was noted that when RAVSAK officially opened up its programs to students in Pardes schools, the optics in front of funders were good. The alliance would officially expand *HaYidion* and add texture to RAVSAK programs. Pardes had some big schools; they had new heads whom RAVSAK could serve. A motion to proceed passed unanimously.

The chair of PEJE contacted RAVSAK's Board Chair Rebekah Farber, as had its executive director. The latter said that PEJE felt strategically aligned with Yeshiva University and that all the organizations should come together to satisfy the demands of the Jim Joseph Foundation. It was suggested that RAVSAK merge with one group at a time. Marc Kramer listed past incidents of conflict with YU and expressed the view that the difference between Orthodox and non-Orthodox institutions was so significant that consolidation into one organization would not work well. Discussion ensued regarding PEJE's programming and offerings, which dealt primarily with the business side and sustainability of day schools. It was noted that funders did not understand why there were different organizations. Due to the complementary nature of the resources PEJE had gathered, the question was why they and RAVSAK could not work together to serve schools. The RAVSAK board members stressed again that RAVSAK needed to ask, at every juncture, what was best for community schools and for the field. While a more streamlined set of services might be beneficial, it would only work if PEJE brought funding. Since PEJE was based in Boston, where all of their staff resided, there might be no financial savings.

Over the next few months, the lay and professional leaders of the five organizations identified areas of commonality/overlap and gaps in desirable services to the field. Shared concerns regarding competition for funding and the potential for economies of scale were noted, although the primary focus was on ensuring that the field of Jewish day school education got the services it needed. A level of mutual trust, notably missing in prior interactions between the organizations, was achieved. This was seen as a solid beginning to the process of identifying areas for collaboration. On a conference call with the AVI CHAI and Jim Joseph foundations, all five organizations spoke with a single voice and affirmed their commitment to a thoughtful process and real collaboration, but not to a pre-determined outcome. It was made clear that the process needed to be owned by the lay and professional leaders of the five organizations with a role for the funders. The impression of the participants was that their report was well received by the foundation officials, who were pleasantly surprised by the accord.

Ongoing work with a consultant surfaced issues facing all five organizations: dependence on a few funding sources; donations not returned to pre-recession levels; adverse impact of recession on ability of families to afford day school education; day schools becoming accustomed to receiving free or subsidized services from organizations serving the field. The professionals saw alignment in programmatic offerings of the organizations and potential for collaboration in expanding and enhancing their offerings. All were focused on achieving sustainable business models.

While the diversity of existing operating practices (governance, staffing, and membership, for example) could create challenges to moving forward together. A vision emerged of a consolidated national entity that was sustained by a diversified revenue base, including both earned and contributed revenue. There was recognition of the desirability of moving along a continuum from increased collaboration toward a single national organization as a longer-term goal. The professionals recommended that the five organizations, through a task force of their lay and professional representatives, undertake a six to eight month planning process that charted the agencies' path toward consolidation. The planning would address the organizational and financial challenges of coming together, and ultimately answer the question, "Will it work?"

At the RAVSAK board's annual meeting in September 2014, Rebekah Farber reported that she had received a call from the chair of the PEJE board. He said that PEJE was looking at a six-month timeline during which they wanted to merge with RAVSAK. PEJE board members felt that RAVSAK and PEJE complemented each other, and they wanted Marc Kramer to head a merged organization which the other organizations could join. How did the RAVSAK board feel about this?

Lengthy and impassioned debate followed. How authentic was the offer? How would it impact discussions with the other organizations? Would it derail the merger process? How would this impact the strategic alliance between Pardes and RAVSAK? Why did the proposed PEJE and YU merger fall apart? What did PEJE bring to the table? Would this force RAVSAK to merge with the other three organizations? Would RAVSAK still exist or would it have a new name? Was there a downside to joining with PEJE? What was the situation with Schechter? It was eventually decided that RAVSAK would express interest and would work with PEJE's timeframe. Conceptually, there was no programmatic overlap. PEJE had an important portfolio of programs for the field that did not impinge on

The Demise of RAVSAK

RAVSAK's mission, vision or values. The difficult issues would be staffing and financing. If RAVSAK combined a merger with PEJE and a consolidation with Pardes, it would have a stronger position vis-a-vis Schechter and YU, although it was stressed that if this went forward, RAVSAK would need to convey to Schechter and YU that a partnership conversation was still needed. There was nothing to do but sit and wait to see what would happen.

New members joined the RAVSAK board. Ann Bennett, past president of Gesher Jewish Day School in Northern Virginia and a board member of the Jewish Federation of Greater Washington, joined in September 2014. In July 2015, attorney Beni Surpin, a partner with Foley & Lardner LLP, became a board member. Surpin's area of focus was on global technology and commercial transactions.

In April 2015, the board created a Plan B task force to think about creating a lean, high-functioning organization dedicated to excellence in Jewish education. The task force attempted to understand what it would take to maintain the core mission of RAVSAK if merger talks failed or if the RAVSAK board voted against a merger. If this occurred, AVI CHAI support would cease and RAVSAK would lose half of its funding. Ann Bennett and Matt Heilicher chaired the task force, which included Elliot Spiegel, Karen Feller, Lesley Zafran, Lisa Breslau, Uri Benhamron, Shira Brown, Beni Surpin, and Marc Kramer. They reported back to the board that they had envisioned a RAVSAK that serviced schools as its top priority and focused on pluralism, leadership, and sustainability, and played in a much larger playground.

Bennett indicated that there were many expert providers servicing these areas with which RAVSAK could collaborate, moving it away from the day school world into a world that was innovative and forward thinking. She said, "We want to continue to be thought leaders and build programs and services that schools need; possibly to be housed elsewhere; with the possibility of exciting new donors and new collaborations. We believe that all schools are concerned about sustainability and will see excellence as a means to greater sustainability." The task force also outlined barriers to success. "We have to understand the risks well and have to determine to the best of our ability if we can overcome them," Bennet said. "We would be very lean in the short term before growing. We're not just selling maintenance of our organization. A bold vision can inspire investment in RAVSAK."

The Spring Report, as it was called, was an audacious and visionary document, outlining a short-term strategic work plan for a year and a half from January 2016 to June 2017. It asserted that the RAVSAK board needed to "make an assertive decision concerning its future not merely because of this organization's past success but rather because of a future imperative. A moment has come when RAVSAK must redefine itself not because it may feel imperiled as an organization but because, through this process of introspection and redefinition, it can better serve the needs of our member schools. It should be the conviction of the board that among those organizations serving the day schools of North America only RAVSAK has the capacity to preserve and deepen both the value of religious diversity which characterizes heterodox day school education, as well as the ability to strengthen quality lay and professional leadership in our schools. It is the position of the Spring Committee that this is a profound trust that cannot be allowed to be compromised."

The Spring Report contextualized RAVSAK's mission within the larger framework of Jewish education in America, stating, "In a sense this decision will have a lasting impact on the future of the Diaspora Jewish community for generations to come. This moment in the history of RAVSAK as an organization coincides with some of the most significant challenges facing the day schools of North America in the last 50 years. Financially strong day schools are becoming ever more sophisticated in their pedagogy and require a network of equally proficient schools with which to interact, while many financially vulnerable schools are in danger of closing their doors and are therefore in need of the wisdom and guidance that RAVSAK provides. As the day school world weighs possible directions to addressing these issues, RAVSAK must choose those solutions that both reflect its substantial expertise as well as its unique vision. RAVSAK has earned a reputation for visionary leadership and it is that gift that must now be redesigned and strengthened in the service of day school education."

The Spring Plan envisioned the creation of three institutes, each of which would focus "on an element of excellence key to the success of our member schools (excellent education; excellent leadership; excellent ways of achieving sustainability), each offering an array of programs and services that stem from a constellation of non-competitive partnerships with organizations and individuals which bring standard bearing content and expertise." The institutes were described as follows:

1. The Jewish Pluralism and Educational Excellence Institute focused on actualizing the Jewish mission of schools to provide an outstanding

Jewish education in settings fully and uniquely committed to serving a diverse and evolving Jewish community.

2. The RAVSAK Leadership Institute focused on leadership development and growth for leaders at administrative, educational, governance, and classroom levels as the driving forces behind school success.

3. The RAVSAK Sustainability Institute dedicated to providing leading-edge thinking, training, advocacy, and support in the domains of school management that ensure institutional vitality. The RAVSAK board received the confidential report and agreed to study its recommendations carefully and seriously.

4.

Operationally, RAVSAK continued to flourish. Elliott Rabin published *eRAVSAK*, a monthly series of online newsletters providing useful information to the field of day school employees. He created a blog called "One Sixtieth of Prophecy," which offered weekly musings exploring areas of potential growth and development in Jewish day schools. RAVSAK published a groundbreaking study, entitled "Heads of Jewish Community Day Schools: A Portrait of the Field." It provided current data on school size and budget, educational and professional backgrounds of heads of school, length of service, salary, gender, and benefit statistics, and perceived strengths and needs of heads.

Apprehension about the possibility of RAVSAK merging or somehow reconfiguring its operations was evident in the field. Two retired heads of school, Karen Feller of Donna Klein Jewish Academy and Elliott Spiegel of the Solomon Schechter School of Westchester, sent a letter to the board of directors expressing concern about the lack of a conference and the possibility that funding would be lost for the head of school mentoring program. They went further, stating, "We are concerned that RAVSAK is in jeopardy of losing its unique mission and ability to serve the day schools of North America. We are concerned that RAVSAK is being pressured to relinquish its special task in seeking the success of day school education. It is as a result of these concerns that we write to you in the shared belief that RAVSAK must continue to serve the cause of day school education. We believe that its mission cannot be duplicated through any joining with other organizations. We fear the dilution of a unique approach to serving our schools. We believe that a record of success ought not to be jeopardized. Our concern does not stem merely from institutional loyalty. Rather, our belief comes from a conviction that the future of the Jewish community is dependent upon the lives of real young men and women, graduates of our schools, who will be educated in the western tradition of open intellectual inquiry, sophisticated in Twenty-first Century challenges, rooted in Jewish social values and comfortable with the text sources of our Jewish and American cultures." They concluded by emphasizing their conviction that "These goals can only be assured through RAVSAK's particular vision and programming which include the preparation of strong visionary Heads of School, the training and support of mature boards of trustees, the encouragement of quality pedagogy, and all within a commitment to the natural diversity of the Jewish community. Only RAVSAK is in a position to pursue and accomplish these goals."

In October, Marc Kramer gave an update on the interagency conversations. He said that the discussion with funders had moved beyond the topics of consolidation and new structure to talking about reorganizing how the field was served. He cited both an operating tension and goal confusion in the session, with the funders seeming to say, "We want to do this better but we don't know how," and "We have a solution and strategy but we are not disclosing it." The professionals felt that the funders did not appreciate the responsibility that the lay and professional leadership of the five organizations had to their respective organizations. In the meantime, the memorandum of understanding that had been sent to Pardes had received no response.

Rebekah Farber continued to feel that she was threading a very thin needle, trying to practice good governance for RAVSAK, doing what was best for the organization, and being between a rock and a hard place with its largest funder. She reported that AVI CHAI staff felt that RAVSAK was not doing what AVI CHAI wanted, was not partnering fully with them, and felt duped, usurped, and blindsided. The board discussed RAVSAK's relationship with AVI CHAI at great length. It was noted that AVI CHAI saw itself as the most important foundation in the Jewish day school world and because they only had five years left, they were very concerned about their legacy. Being independent of them would be beneficial, converting them to a program funder, but RAVSAK needed to raise funds sustainably, not just for a year. The question was posed: Should we be more grateful for their support? AVI CHAI believed that they saw the bigger picture and that RAVSAK did not. Discussion ensued about the dangers of involving them but then not doing what they ask; about the likelihood of their being punitive; about the wisdom of having them be too involved and too directive; and about the difficulty of raising the kind of funds necessary for RAVSAK to continue.

The board concluded that it had to stay on mission, listen to RAVSAK's constituents, and do what they wanted and needed. RAVSAK was a connector and needed to stay true to that and not just do what funders demanded. Farber concluded that RAVSAK needed to be self-reflective, to stay in touch with and serve the needs of its constituents, and to be very careful about relationships with funders. The board was aware of AVI CHAI's concern about RAVSAK "going rogue." It was decided to let AVI CHAI know that RAVSAK was delaying its plans for a CEO until there was greater clarity with regard to the interagency conversations. The importance of reaching an agreement with Pardes was stressed.

Idana Goldberg was promoted to RAVSAK's co-executive director in 2015. Membership had reached an all-time high of 138 schools. Funding to sustain RAVSAK as an independent entity, however, was still not forthcoming, and the organization continued to struggle to meet the development goals specified in its business plan. Goldberg was tasked to take on the institutional advancement portfolio. Although it was not her primary area of expertise, she was willing to do so to support the organization. In December 2015, Lesley Zafran delivered a prophetic *d'var Torah* to the board, concluding: "For the past year, our Board has been wrestling with change. Whatever the future holds, there will be change. Change feels scary. Whether we are 'in' or 'out', we will need fresh ways of defining ourselves and must be willing to face change as we go forward into uncharted territory. May G-d always be by our side as we undertake our upcoming task with eyes open, questioning and discerning minds, and integrity of heart and spirit."

A document entitled "Advancing Jewish Day Schools, the Field, and our Future," drafted by LaPiana Consulting on behalf of the "Jewish Day School Consolidation Initiative" then appeared. It was described as an "Integration Business Plan," the purpose of which was "to describe the vision, mission, strategy, structure, operations, and financial model for a new, centralized, North American Jewish day school organization." Because the proposed entity was not yet named, it was referred to as "NewOrg." The plan described the current reality of the day school world: "Reflective of the broader Jewish community, [day] schools have evolved according to their specific understanding of Judaism and its practices and rituals. As a result, schools have identified with a particular denominational or ideological perspective (Community schools, Reform schools, Conservative schools, and Orthodox schools). Over time, organizations arose to support these schools as they sought to achieve educational excellence and financial strength. Primarily focused on a specific denomination/ideological perspective or 'stream,' these organizations have provided an array of services and supports to segments of the day school community."

The document explained the basic premise on which the proposed consolidation was based: "While historically able to serve schools successfully, the opportunity to combine their skills and experience and broaden their impact across specific identities, along with a changing funding environment, have led the leadership of these organizations to conclude that bringing together the best of what each organization offers—and combining that with innovative new resources, services, technologies, and approaches that leverage the many lessons learned across the field over more than twenty years—has unparalleled potential to sustain and enhance the Jewish day school field."[2] Three measures of success were specified: 1. Jewish day schools will become stronger and more vibrant Jewish communal institutions; 2. Jewish day schools will play a central role in the lives of students, families, and the community as a whole; and 3. Jewish day schools will contribute to the development of a modern, highly educated, and dynamic Jewish community that is steeped in Judaism's cherished traditions, active in its contributions to Jewish life, and energetically engaged in the religious, academic, and secular issues of the day.

The report acknowledged that the plan reflected a significant transformation of the founding organizations into a new, integrated entity, and that "this level of change brings with it inherent risks, some that can be predicted and some that cannot." It stressed, however, that the planning team had worked hard to identify these risks and to develop a plan for managing and mitigating them as part of the transition and implementation of NewOrg. It concluded that the business plan "sets out a blueprint for the successful creation of a new, integrated North American organization. It is intended as a set of guidelines for the board, CEO, and staff, who will be responsible for continually refining the plan based on current realities and information, as well as their best judgment. Armed with this plan, they will be well-positioned to build an organization that provides maximum benefit

---

2. LaPiana, "Advancing,"

The Demise of RAVSAK

to day schools and the field, and does so in a way that creates financial strength for both Jewish day schools and the new organization."

The RAVSAK board was deeply conflicted about the new entity. As it debated whether to go "all in" with the merger plan, the following negative points were surfaced:

1. There was no guaranteed funding yet from any source other than AVI CHAI.
2. No business plan had been made available to potential funders and no commitments had been requested when funders were surveyed.
3. There was a guaranteed $1.5 million deficit after three years unless someone stepped up to fill AVI CHAI's funding line; there was currently no "succession plan" for AVI CHAI's funding.
4. The CEO was not yet identified and his/her ability to fundraise was not known.
5. Donors were already expecting to be involved with the organization as a condition of their philanthropy; depending on who these donors were, this could be problematic for community schools.
6. There were significant expenses involved in closing down the operations of intermediaries and there would be an immediate need for cash when the new organization began.
7. There was the possibility of losing the RAVSAK executives.
8. There was a real question about the viability of a merger of Orthodox and non-Orthodox associations, especially with regard to the issue of pluralism.

Reasons for going "all in" included the following:

1. RAVSAK had no guaranteed funding from any new sources; the elimination of AVI CHAI funding would put it in a disastrous financial situation.
2. There was donor and board fatigue.
3. RAVSAK had not had a record of success in attracting funding.
4. It was not known how many RAVSAK schools would defect to NewOrg. It was unrealistic to expect schools to stay with RAVSAK if NewOrg offered the same services at lower or no cost.

5. There would be bad press if RAVSAK refused to join with the other agencies.

In the end, board members believed that the merger was about more than just RAVSAK and that not to go in was to break faith with RAVSAK schools. The energy around the initiative and the distribution of leadership coming from that collective energy was seen as positive. It was acknowledged that there were a lot of unknowns and that there was grieving. One board member said, "I think this will be 'good for the Jews,' although I am saddened by the change of something that I thought was unique and precious." There was an awareness of the risks both of going in and of not going in, but a belief that pragmatism needed to prevail. The board was confident in the people involved in the merger and believed that when intelligent and well-meaning people are involved, organizations have a good chance for success. A single entity would be a magnet for good people.

On January 12, 2016, the following resolutions were presented to the RAVSAK board:

> 1. The Board of Directors of Jewish Community Day School Network, Inc., doing business as RAVSAK ("RAVSAK"), approves moving forward toward forming this strategic affiliation, based on the terms contained in the Summary of Agreements outlined below and attached hereto, pending negotiation of the terms of, and approval of, a binding agreement between the Intermediaries and all legal documents necessary to effectuate such transaction.
>
> 2. The Board of Directors of RAVSAK shall take all prudent steps, including the conduct of due diligence and negotiation of terms, without delay and with the expectation that RAVSAK shall execute any and all final legal agreements necessary to effectuate the terms of the affiliation outlined in these resolutions and the accompanying Summary of Agreements in anticipation of launching NewOrg on or as close to July 1, 2016 as possible.

The vote was twelve in favor; one opposed.

On January 19, a press release was issued by The AVI CHAI Foundation, announcing the realization of a vision of a more unified field of Jewish day schools through the formation of a new combined day school organization to be known as NewOrg until a name was finalized. "NewOrg is committed to improving financial vitality and educational excellence in Jewish day schools, and supporting a vibrant, visible and connected Jewish day school field," the release stated. "It will work directly with schools, cohorts of schools, and individual professional and lay leaders to strengthen skills and build capacity in areas of teaching and learning, leadership, governance, affordability, recruitment, retention, fund development and endowment building. As an integrated organization serving and strengthening all streams of Jewish day schools, it will work on advancing the Jewish day school field across North America as well as on advocacy efforts for day schools locally and regionally. NewOrg will promote greater communal and funder engagement with local day schools, and will work with schools and communities to strengthen enrollment." It further declared that AVI CHAI had pledged financial support to advance the work of NewOrg and intended to remain a consistent funder of the organization until the foundation's sunset in 2019.

In a joint statement, the Planning Team said, "The formation of a single integrated day school organization will optimize the quality of services we provide to the schools we serve, giving them the resources they need to build the strongest possible future. It is a definitive affirmation of the centrality of day schools in Jewish life and reflects our dedication to seeing Jewish learning, literacy, culture, and commitment flourish in a rapidly changing world. At the same time, this joint plan and decision reflects the conviction of many in the day school community that we can all benefit from the knowledge, expertise and ideas of others, even if we express our Jewishness differently. As one organization, we can unify to strengthen day schools, what we believe to be the core of the Jewish educational enterprise." It stated that the Planning Team had initiated a global search for a Chief Executive Officer to lead the new organization, that initial board of directors would be built from its current core of one representative from each of the organizations, as well as from AVI CHAI, and that a branding process had begun to select the new organization's name and develop an identity that reflected a unified, cooperative, and fresh vision for the Jewish day school field. Shortly thereafter, it was announced that NewOrg would henceforth be called Prizmah: Center for Jewish Day Schools.

On February 17, 2016, newly-elected Board Chair Kathy Manning sent an email to schools saying that "Combining the resources, knowledge, skills and commitment of their organizations will result in a new organization that will be greater than the sum of its parts—a stronger, more efficient resource for the hundreds of wonderful day schools across North America." She explained that she had already begun working with Jewish community leaders who represented the six organizations which had merged to become

NewOrg: Dara Yanowitz (Schechter), Jodi Hessel (PARDES), Joseph Steiner (RAVSAK), Michael Bohnen (PEJE), Nathan Lindenbaum (YUSP) and Yossi Prager (AVI CHAI); Yehuda Neuberger also joined the board. AVI CHAI funding would cease On May 19, a press release announced the selection of Paul Bernstein as the organization's founding chief executive officer and a $2 million grant from the Jim Joseph Foundation.

The RAVSAK board met in New York City for the last time on June 23 and June 24, 2016. Paul Bernstein, Prizmah's CEO, addressed the members. He said he was hoping that NewOrg would be the sum of the parts or something much larger "to justify the pain you've gone through to get here." He saw this as a chance to build on incredible foundations. Although he was not a professional educator, he said, he wanted to have the right educators on the team because he believed in the importance of the quality of education coming first. He stated that the NewOrg vision needed to emerge but that he had two priorities: working hard on team and staffing questions, and learning from all the people in order to inform the vision. He was an optimist for the Jewish community, he continued, but was pessimistic about the lack of vision in the NewOrg world. He expressed the belief that school quality was the factor that most influenced enrollment and that part of the issue related to quality is that schools function on the same model as they did twenty years ago. He asked how innovative high quality programming could be brought to schools and said that he saw the potential for a 100 percent improvement in what schools do. Bernstein concluded saying that there was a high level of engagement on the NewOrg board and that they needed to explore how to build networks and communities, find the right engagement points, and figure out the right people and places to engage. "I am keen to continue the conversation," he closed, "We are standing on your shoulders."

On June 30, 2016, RAVSAK officially ended its thirty-sixth year and, pending approval of the New York State Attorney General, became part of a new organization named Prizmah: Center for Jewish Day Schools, dedicated to serving Jewish day schools in powerful and sustainable ways. At that point, RAVSAK: the Jewish Community Day School Network, ceased to exist, and the future of the community day school movement as a singular and cohesive entity was up in the air.

7

Challenges of the Jewish Community Day School Network

Dialogue, openness to another point of view, respect for diversity—these are sorely lacking in our world.[1]

SAUL WACHS

WHETHER THE HEBREW ACRONYM RAVSAK or its English translation, Jewish Community Day School Network, is used, the conflicts inherent in the community day school movement are embedded within the organization's very name. Jewish: which definition of Judaism applies? Community: who are a community school's constituents, supporters, and allies? Day School: why do Jewish parents overwhelmingly opt for public school? Network: can the affinity, accord and mutual understanding that bound together the heads and lay leaders of community day schools since the inception of JCDSN/RAVSAK survive in the face of the current divisions within the Jewish world?

These issues are all inextricably linked to the deep schisms within the Jewish world regarding *Klal Yisrael* and pluralism. Community day schools, committed to this concept, are *ipso facto* fully engaged with it. But the major conflict dividing American Jews in the twenty-first century that

1. Wachs, "Devar Torah," Para. 16.

directly impacts their commitment or lack of commitment to intensive Jewish education, as provided by day schools, involves pluralism in two main ways: 1. integration with *vs* isolation from secular society, and 2. inclusivity *vs* exclusivity with respect to women, children of interfaith marriage and patrilineal descent, and members of the LGBTQ community.

Jewish: Which definition of Judaism applies?

The community day school stands at the crux of the existential dilemma facing the American Jewish community at the beginning of the twenty-first century: Does it align with the ultra-Orthodox model of rejecting modernity, the larger community, and the siren calls of technology, science, social media, and the arts? Or does it risk abandoning its understanding of Judaism by embracing those very -isms—pluralism, feminism, individualism, egalitarianism, liberalism—that seemingly run counter to *halacha* as it has traditionally been understood and observed?

The division can be seen in the differences between the Orthodox day school world and the community day school world. Yet, as Susan Kardos has noted, the biggest challenge is not facing day schools, it faces the Jewish community as a whole. "It's the crisis in moving toward more and more bifurcation within our own people, with Orthodox on one side and non-Orthodox on the other. Intensive and immersive Jewish education doesn't seem to be as consistently important to the non-Orthodox sector," Kardos observed. "There's a center within the Jewish people which is falling out. I think that center serves as a critical bridge between the two poles. The more that falls out, the greater tragedy it is for the Jewish people, since it limits the sense of access to and ownership of our tradition, history, and sacred text within non-Orthodox communities."[2]

Beginning in 1983, the 1,000-member Rabbinical Council of America (RCA) began to issue rulings that clearly delineated the schism that existed between Orthodox and non-Orthodox Judaism and that directly and squarely placed Orthodoxy on a collision course with community day schools in three key areas:

1. Patrilineal descent and interfaith families: In response to the Central Conference of American Rabbis' ruling that the child of one Jewish parent is under the presumption of Jewish descent, the Rabbinical Council declared: "Jewish identity by birth throughout the ages has been determined by all Jews as deriving from the Jewishness of the

---

2. Kardos, "Who's Who," Para. 8.

natural mother. This principle has preserved the unity of the Jewish people. Therefore, the Rabbinical Council of America deplores and denounces the resolution adopted by the Central Conference of American Rabbis at its recent convention that the Jewish identity of the child can be determined by patrilineal descent. This action of the Central Conference of American Rabbis is destroying the oneness of the Jewish people and publicly inviting and encouraging intermarriage. A child born to a non-Jewish mother is not Jewish and no statement to the contrary can legitimize its Jewish identity."[3] The Rabbinical Council urged the Central Conference of American Rabbis to reverse "this deplorable decision,"[4] and called upon its president to appoint committees to "to educate the Jewish community to the schismatic nature and dangerous implications of the recent patrilineal resolution adopted by the CCAR" and "to take whatever steps are necessary to guarantee the Halachic integrity of the Jewish family."[5]

2. Same-sex marriage: In 2004 the RCA and the Union of Orthodox Jewish Congregations of America issued a statement of principle on same-sex marriage that firmly and unambiguously stated that "Homosexual behavior is, and has always been, absolutely forbidden by Jewish law and tradition. Any attempt to characterize Jewish law and tradition to the contrary must be rejected. The only legitimate form of sexual behavior is that which takes place between adult men and women, within the sacred institution of marriage, as traditionally defined and permitted. Under no circumstances can Jewish tradition or law countenance a notion of so-called 'same sex marriage' rituals or status under religious auspices. . . The institution of marriage, and family life, as defined and practiced for thousands of years as between a man and a woman, a father and a mother, respectively, is far too important and essential to the bedrock of society and civilization as we know it, to be thus undermined by those who presume to redefine its essence."[6] In 2006 the RCA noted with regret the decisions of the Rabbinical Assembly of the Conservative movement to permit the ordination of gays and lesbians and to permit rabbis to officiate at same-sex commitment ceremonies (marriages where permitted by

3. Rabbinical Council, "Patrilineal Descent," Para. 3.
4. Rabbinical Council, "Patrilineal Descent," Para. 4.
5. Rabbinical Council, "Patrilineal Descent," Para. 5.
6. Rabbinical Council, "Response," Para. 6.

law.) The RCA declared "This decision represents yet another significant step in the further estrangement of the Conservative movement from Jewish law (halachah) and tradition. Homosexual behavior is a clear and unambiguous biblical prohibition. The attempts to formulate halachic license or creative interpretation to permit prohibited behavior should not mislead anyone committed to traditional Judaism, into thinking that there can be any permissibility to homosexual activity, whether by rabbis or laypersons. And thus, to permit those who openly proclaim their nonadherence to Torah law, to assume positions of rabbinic leadership, is an entirely regrettable step. We are also saddened by the concurrent decision of the Rabbinical Assembly to permit same sex 'commitment ceremonies' which undermine the institution of Jewish marriage and Jewish family life."[7] "Regrettably," the RCA concluded, "these decisions will in the end serve to further deepen the schisms within the Jewish people."[8]

3. Gender equality: In 2015, the RCA passed a resolution stating that "RCA members with positions in Orthodox institutions may not ordain women into the Orthodox rabbinate, regardless of the title used; or hire or ratify the hiring of a woman into a rabbinic position at an Orthodox institution; or allow a title implying rabbinic ordination to be used by a teacher"[9] in an Orthodox institution. Rabbi Shalom Baum, RCA's president, described the group's opposition to the ordination of women as "overwhelming," although in a separate letter he added that "as we move forward, we must ensure that women's voices are heard and respected."[10][/NL]

There are Jews for whom the following paragraph lacks both meaning and relevance:

> *Maran (Shulhan Aruch 253:5) discusses reheating a food called 'panadish' on Shabbat. He rules that it is permissible to return such a dish to the blech even though it has cooled off because it is a solid, fully cooked food. However, the Mishna Berura (Rav Yisrael Meir Kagan, 1839–1933) points out that if this dish contains a significant amount of congealed fat, it would be forbidden to reheat it, because*

---

7. Rabbinical Council, "Response," Para. 2.
8. Rabbinical Council, "Response," Para. 4.
9. Rabbinical Council, "RCA Policy," Para. 3.
10. Rabbinical Council, "RCA Passes," Para. 4.

> the solid fat will melt into a liquid. This constitutes the prohibition of Nolad, creating a new form of a substance. Maran, however, in Siman 318:16 clearly states that it is permitted to reheat a dish called 'empanada' even though it also contains congealed fat which will melt. Evidently, he holds that there is no problem of Nolad. The prohibition of Nolad is only present if one actively intervened to change the form of the food. For example, crushing ice with one's hands and transforming it to water would be a problem of Nolad.[11]

There are also Jews for whom these are matters of grave concern. And therein lies the problem. As Avi Weiss and Rella Fellman wrote, "On the one hand, there are those who focus on boundaries, fences, high and thick—obsessing and spending inordinate amounts of time ostracizing, condemning, and declaring who is beyond the pale,"[12] while on the other hand, there are those who take an alternative approach. Orthodox Judaism has always avoided dialogue and religious interaction with non-Orthodox Jews. But in the twenty-first century, the definition of non-Orthodox has been expanded substantially and positions *vis-à-vis* other Jews have hardened considerably. The Orthodox community is in the process of drastically redefining its relationship to the modern world. Over the past several decades, Orthodox Judaism has moved further and further to the right. In addition to notably more stringent observance of *halacha*, this Haredization has resulted in enforced separation not only from the non-Jewish world but also from rest of the Jewish world, whether secular, Reform, Conservative or Modern Orthodox.

Yitz Greenberg commented on the Pew survey statistic that Orthodoxy had grown from 7.7 percent of the national Jewish population in 1990 to 10 percent. "Most dramatic," Greenberg pointed out, "was that unlike in 1960 when the dominant Orthodox defined themselves as modern, in 2014 two-thirds of the Orthodox described themselves as Charedi and only one-third as modern. To put it another way: the modern Orthodox cohort had fallen from 14–15 percent of the national Jewish population to 3 percent — this, at the same time that a number of the main modern institutions had been co-opted to follow policies that favored Charedi culture but weakened modern Orthodox viability."[13] But an even more critical division between modern, centrist, and open Orthodox schools and community

---

11. Mansour, "Reheating," Para. 1.
12 Weiss and Fellman, "Inclusive," Para. 10.
13. Greenberg, "Can Modern Orthodoxy," Para. 23.

day schools is the issue of pluralism. David Wolpe explained that "What Orthodoxy requires is precisely what Conservative and Reform Judaism reject. Unity for the Orthodox can mean nothing more than inclusion: The non-Orthodox are wrong, but still Jewish. Unity for liberal Jews, however, means pluralism [i.e. open to the thoughts and ideas of each denomination], even allowing for significant differences between the Conservative and Reform movements. The Orthodox must affirm the legitimacy of non-Orthodox ideologies as authentically Jewish. But this is precisely what the Orthodox cannot do."[14]

Who defines Jewish? "The number of Jews in the world is smaller than a small statistical error in the Chinese census,"[15] wrote sociographer Milton Himmelfarb. "Among Americans of all kinds, moreover, Jews have the fewest number of siblings, the smallest household size, and the second lowest number of children under eighteen at home,"[16] wrote demographer Jack Wertheimer. Yet this tiny group of people seems to spend an inordinate amount of time trying to reduce the number of its own adherents by disowning one another. The Jewish community seems to have arrived at the sorry state described in Irving Greenberg's monograph *Will There Be One Jewish People in the Year 2000?*: "In the past, anti-Semites built their plans on the expectation and hope that the Jews will disappear. We have come to a tragic situation where good and committed Jews are predicating their survival strategies on the disappearance of other Jews."[17]

Historian Jonathan Sarna pointed out that the Jewish diaspora has shrunk by more than forty percent since 1939 and that 95 percent of world Jewry is confined to just fourteen countries today. Only thirty-nine countries can boast communities of 5,000 or more Jews. "Most of the 200 or so countries of the world, including several where Jews had lived for millennia (Iraq, Syria, Ethiopia)" wrote Sarna, "are now completely barren of Jews or show tiny communities that are unsustainable. Indeed, huge areas of the world show no Jewish presence whatsoever."[18] This is the environment in which community day schools function. Committed to transideological Jewish education, they and they alone acknowledge the validity of all major streams of Jewish thought and the incorporation of this principle into

---

14. Wolpe, "Chief Rabbi's Achievement," Para. 3.
15. Himmelfarb, "In the light," Para. 69.
16. Wertheimer, "Jews and Birthrate," Para. 8.
17. Greenberg, *Will There Be*, 4.
18. Sarna, *American Jews*, 4.

the curricula of their schools. This acknowledgement implies that there exist many possible options for the expression of Judaism. Community day schools prize, appreciate, and advocate for the value concept of *Klal Yisrael* and promote participation in Jewish community life, regardless of its ideological basis.

It is not up to schools to define who or what is Jewish. "While some communities are based on sameness and aspirations of homogeneity," writes Rabbi Mitchel Malkus, "pluralistic schools and communities center around the awareness of others, multiple viewpoints, practices and beliefs, and the interdependence of all community members."[19] Community day schools by definition prize diversity, open-mindedness, mutual understanding, and acceptance of difference. In the twenty-first century, with a shrinking world Jewish population, the time has come to accept that we cannot all speak the same language (as the story of the Tower of Babel tells us) nor can we all be the same (there were, after all, twelve tribes), but we can follow the lesson inherent in Jacob's blessing of his sons ("everyone according to his blessing he blessed them" [Gen. 49:28]) and recognize the vital role that community day schools, which value *Klal Yisrael* so highly, are positioned to play in the twenty-first century. Jewish education has to keep pace with a world in which everyone is connected, homes and offices are "smart" and voice-activated, robots and drones conduct wars, bots affect elections, and sensors can monitor everything we do. Do we need, in this environment, to expend precious Jewish energy defining who we are?

Community: Who are community schools' constituents?

The lack of promotion of community day schools from the non-Orthodox rabbinate is one of the great tragedies of the day school movement. It is ironic that in the face of all evidence that day schools are effective not only in terms of educational excellence but in producing committed Jewish leaders for the Jewish community, there is an almost a total lack of support for them among the very members of the community leadership who should be their strongest advocates. While one would assume that rabbis would be the natural allies of day schools, fervently desirous of having well-educated, learned, capable, and observant congregations, the opposite seems to be true. Very few congregational rabbis outside of the Orthodox world speak in favor of day school education. Some see this as an unwillingness to champion anything other than their own synagogues' supplementary schools, which hold children and their families captive (and

---

19. Malkus, "What defines," Para. 3.

paying dues) at least until bar/t mitzvah or confirmation. Others believe that rabbis prefer congregants who are minimally conversant with the faith and therefore reliant upon the clergy in these matters. Even in the Reform and Conservative movements, which have their own day school networks, rabbinical support is tepid. And the silence of rabbis in communities where neither a Pardes nor a Schechter school exists in competition with a community day school is still deafening.

"Where are the pulpit rabbis?" asked businessman and philanthropist George Hanus, one of the very few day school advocates to publicly excoriate the rabbinate on the issue of day schools. "They sermonize about every imaginable social topic except providing free high-quality Jewish day school education for all children who seek it regardless of their religious affiliation or family financial condition. Why?"[20] The answer to this question lies in the prominence of the bar/t mitzvah in American Jewish family life, which is so consequential that the congregational rabbi, in whose synagogue the event must be held, has become the power player in the contest for control of Jewish education. Though day schools are often a must for their own children, and they would not move to a community without a day school, rabbis sing a different tune for their congregants' children, for whom the congregational school is considered not only "good enough" but even preferable. There are several reasons for their position: Congregational schools require congregational affiliation. Since the 1950s, synagogue affiliation has been the principal means by which Americans voluntarily associated with Judaism although that association is diminishing significantly in the twenty-first century. And membership, particularly young membership, is a vital determinant of a rabbi's success. The second reason is simple economics: the more students in a congregational school, the less the per pupil cost. Third, if a child is enrolled in a day school, there is always the fear (though no data to support it) that a day school family will not affiliate with a synagogue.

These are issues that are easily resolved and that pale before the larger issue of the value of an immersive and life-defining Jewish education. When Rabbi Jay Moses, vice president of the Wexner Foundation, examined the reason that synagogues and day schools do not collaborate for their mutual benefit, he noted that, "Our institutions are not built to collaborate. The structure and culture of synagogues promote competition. Potential members go 'synagogue shopping' and ultimately pay dues and contribute to the

---

20. Hanus, "Where," Para. 7.

viability of one synagogue over all the others. Given that reality, rabbis and synagogue leaders understandably have their identities and egos (to say nothing of their budgets and salaries) tied up in the notion of being 'better' and more attractive than other synagogues."[21] If like-purposed institutions can't work together, what chance do day schools have?

Still, one would hope that the clerical leadership of the non-Orthodox Jewish world would find common ground with their Orthodox counterparts in extolling day school education. It has been vital to the success of the Haredi community and has had equally positive effects in the more liberal sectors. *What Difference Does Day School Make?*, a 2007 study of day school alumni commissioned by the Partnership for Excellence in Jewish Education (PEJE), found that their Jewish day school education provided excellent preparation for a broad range of colleges and universities, including the most selective, and that day school alumni participated in all aspects of undergraduate life and were well represented in the ranks of student leaders. They were more resistant than their public school peers to social pressures such as heavy drinking that lead to other risky behaviors. They were more likely to restrict their dating to Jewish peers and to be involved with Jewish life, learning, observance, Israel and Jewish cultural activities on campus. They were also more likely to demonstrate a stronger sense of responsibility towards addressing the needs of the larger society by influencing social values, helping those in need, and volunteering time to social change efforts.

It is certainly understandable that rabbis are human and have jobs and families to worry about, but as the people most responsible for assuring a viable future for their congregations and for the Jewish people, one can only wonder why they do not respond enthusiastically and without reservation to Rabbi Lord Jonathan Sacks' assertion that "If you want to save the Jewish future, you have to build Jewish day schools – there is no other way."[22] And as Rabbi Eddie Shostak wrote, after conversing with Rabbi Sacks on this topic: "If our shuls are going to be successful, our schools need to be successful. And if our schools are going to be successful, our shuls need to be successful. Not independently, but in partnership."[23]

The second communal cohort that would be expected to back day schools unreservedly are Jewish federations. Yet most federations, though

---

21. Moses, "Learning," 23.
22. Fishman, "Rabbi Jonathan Sacks," Para. 5.
23. Shostak, "School or Shul," Para. 10.

they generally provide some level of financial assistance, are sadly lacking in enthusiasm for day schools. Rather than championing a wellspring of future educated, committed, and enthusiastic leadership of Jewish communities, the lay guardians of Jewish communities' future generally ignore, provide token aid, or are actively hostile to the day schools in their communities, regardless of whether the schools are affiliated with a denomination or are community schools. The lack of support from local federations has undermined the day school movement since its inception. In 1949 a resolution at the Torah Umesorah convention denounced the refusal of many Jewish Federations to allocate funds for the day schools in their communities. The July 26, 1963 Los Angeles *B'nai Brith Messenger* published a strong condemnation of federations declaring their leadership to be "shortsighted and sorely lacking in vision" for failing to recognize the importance of Jewish education in "the struggle for Jewish survival." "Day Schools should not be placed in the position of begging at the door of our Federations," it declared, avowing "Federations must stop issuing pious statements about education and start issuing cash." But federations resisted changing their posture, even in the face of mounting evidence of "the manifest failure of the one-day-a-week and afternoon schools."[24] In 1971, Max Fischer, then president of the Council of Jewish Federations and Welfare Funds, urged communal leaders to re-examine their obligations to the day schools, declaring that "The day school holds one of the very best answers to further Jewish continuity and has earned our most careful consideration of what could be done to help.'"[25] His plea fell on deaf ears.

In 1988 the Commission on Jewish Education in North America was established "to launch an unprecedented undertaking—to pool the energies and resources of all sectors of the Jewish community in a mutual effort to enlarge the scope, raise the standards, and improve the quality of Jewish education."[26] The Commission, a partnership convened by the Mandel Associated Foundations, the JCC Association, and JESNA in collaboration with the Council of Jewish Federations, met for a two-year period. It included Jewish community leaders, scholars, educators, rabbis, leaders of the Orthodox, Conservative, Reconstructionist, and Reform denominations, and the heads of major foundations.

---

24. Ackerman, "Jewish Education," 16
25. Cited in Ackerman, "Jewish Education," 80.
26. Commission on Jewish Education, *Time*, 1.

Challenges of the Jewish Community Day School

The Commission's 1990 report, *A Time to Act*, stated emphatically that "the Jewish community of North America is facing a crisis of major proportions. Large numbers of Jews have lost interest in Jewish values, ideals, and behavior, and there are many who no longer believe that Judaism has a role to play in their search for personal fulfillment and communality. This has grave implications, not only for the richness of Jewish life, but for the very continuity of a large segment of the Jewish people. Over the last several decades, intermarriage between Jews and non-Jews has risen dramatically, and a major proportion of children of such marriages no longer identify themselves as Jews. It is clear that there is a core of deeply committed Jews whose very way of life ensures meaningful Jewish continuity from generation to generation. However, there is a much larger segment of the Jewish population which is finding it increasingly difficult to define its future in terms of Jewish values and behavior."[27] Their conclusion was bold: "The responsibility for developing Jewish identity and instilling a commitment to Judaism for this population now rests primarily with education."[28] The statement could not have been stronger: "Throughout history Jews have faced dangers from without with courage and steadfastness; now a new kind of commitment is required. The Jews of North America live in an open society that presents an unprecedented range of opportunities and choices. This extraordinary environment confronts us with what is proving to be an historic dilemma: while we cherish our freedom as individuals to explore new horizons, we recognize that this very freedom poses a dramatic challenge to the future of the Jewish way of life. The Jewish community must meet the challenge at a time when young people are not sure of their roots in the past or of their identity in the future. There is an urgent need to explore all possible ways to ensure that Jews maintain and strengthen the commitments that are central to Judaism.[29]

The report reviewed the focus the organized Jewish community had placed in the past on other matters: financial support for indigent newcomers and their Americanization; health and social services and problems of anti-Semitism; post-war Jewish relief, rehabilitation, and reconstruction; the building the State of Israel; the development of communal services in North America and the rescue and resettlement of Soviet Jewry, and allowed that "In the face of such life-and-death issues, the needs of education have

---

27. Commission on Jewish Education, *Time*, 15.
28. Commission on Jewish Education, *Time*, 15.
29. Commission on Jewish Education, *Time*, 25.

seemed to be less urgent, less insistent, more diffused; a problem that could be dealt with at some point in the future when more pressing problems have been solved."[30] But now, it asserted, the Jewish community must stop this posturing. "We may continue to live with emergencies indefinitely," the report affirmed, "but we can no longer postpone addressing the needs of Jewish education, lest we face an irreversible decline in the vitality of the Jewish people."[31] Instead of voting on the resolution, however, federation officials decided to form a task force comprised of national federation leaders and representatives from day school advocacy groups and foundations. Once again, nothing happened. At the close of the millennium, a 1997 study by PEJE found that on average, local federations provided only five percent of the funds needed to educate a child in a day school.

Another effort to prioritize Jewish day school education was initiated in 1997 by George Hanus and the National Jewish Day School Scholarship Committee, a coalition of representatives from Chicago-area day schools. The Jewish Federation of Metropolitan Chicago became the first federation in the country to formally endorse the committee's resolution and objectives. Hanus, chair of the newly established Chicago-based group that had focused communal attention on the rising cost of day-school education, hailed the move as a much-needed step in the right direction. The resolution reaffirmed the community's commitment to make a quality day school education available to all Jewish children whose families desire it, including those whose families did not have the necessary financial resources. Hanus hoped to have the resolution passed by the Council of Jewish Federations at its annual meeting, as well as by individual federations across the country. His action, which he described as a deliberate and methodical process to ensure that one of most crucial issues of the day was addressed, was directed at trying to create an absolutely clear record of where contemporary Jewish leaders stand on the issue. An article in the *Jewish News of Northern California* quotes Hanus as asking, "Is Jewish day school education an entitlement, a privilege, a luxury or a right?"

The resolution was put before the General Assembly of the Council of Jewish Federations by the Jewish Federation of Metropolitan Chicago and the Chicago-based National Jewish Day School Scholarship Committee. It proposed that each community "fulfill its commitment to Jewish day school education with dedication and resources consistent with its significant

---

30. Commission on Jewish Education, *Time,* 25.
31. Commission on Jewish Education, *Time,* 25.

importance to the survival of the Jewish community." The resolution was met with immediate resistance and not surprisingly, the response to the proposed resolution was the creation of a task force of thirty-nine people, including national federation leadership, representatives from day school advocacy groups, and foundations, including AVI CHAI and the Partnership for Excellence in Jewish Education. The driving force behind the 1997 resolution, George Hanus of Chicago, participated in the task force and praised its report but expressed skepticism about its impact. He was certainly correct in his assessment.

At the beginning of the new century, the impact and importance of Jewish day schools in the Jewish community began to receive some grudging recognition in the federation world. Surveys were conducted to assess federated support for day school education and to collect data about day schools in communities outside of large metropolitan areas. The results were surprising to many, even as the resulting conclusions and reports were admittedly skewed against smaller and Orthodox schools, which did not even have the resources necessary to complete the surveys or apply for matching grants.

The other "elephant in the room" of challenges faced by the Jewish community day school movement was the intervention of Jewish philanthropy. The 1990 National Jewish Population Survey identified three areas of grave concern: declining levels of Jewish identification and affiliation, rising rates of intermarriage, and disillusionment with the Jewish establishment. It found one possible solution to these dire straits in the rise of large donors and family foundations that challenged existing communal priorities. There is no question that the Jewish community needed the assistance of the philanthropic community, which had the resources to address many of the problems that bedeviled it. The timing was right. "In the 21st century, we can now clearly see a new paradigm of a world characterized by human networks that can upend governments or fund game-changing products; an unbounded start-it-yourself and share-it-with-others ethos; and heightened influence of lone individuals, ephemeral crowds, and enduring social networks," wrote Rabbi Hayim Herring. "Individuals and relatively small groups have the means to effectuate great changes."[32] "Through the early 1990's," he elaborated, "the major funding stream for Jewish programs and infrastructure was the national federation system. In the early 1990's, 'mega'

---

32. Herring," Educating Rabbis," Para. 10.

and family foundations began to provide a massive infusion of funds into new and established organizations that better reflected their interests."[33]

In an interesting 2006 analysis entitled *Philanthropic Lessons from Mapping Jewish Education*, Amy L. Sales clearly and succinctly delineated the fundamental problem with philanthropic efforts in the field of Jewish education: "The Jewish educational system in the United States is a quintessentially American invention that reflects the diversity of the Jewish population and the American context in which it lives. The system has a vast infrastructure and is, perhaps, a 'system' in name only. Though impressive, its size and structure point to an impulse to proliferate programs, create new organizations, and build facilities without tackling the community's fundamental educational challenges. There is little empirical evidence that the system is effective in meeting the challenges entailed in preparing a new generation of engaged Jews."[34] Sales found a disproportionate emphasis on programming versus capacity building (defined as professional development, curriculum development, financial resource development, planning, research, and evaluation) with the result that in all areas of Jewish education "issues of professional competence are pervasive."[35]

Jack Wertheimer observed that "On the positive side, foundations and philanthropists can move quickly and adroitly to address needs; they also have shown some capacity to plan creatively rather than rely on old models."[36] But then he revealed the downside. "The maverick nature of foundations, however, reduces coordination," he wrote. "As a result, educational institutions are left uncertain about how to plan for the future; and when they lose foundation support they tend to lack the capacity to continue programs on their own. Hence the Jewish-education field is littered with experimental programs briefly supported and then abandoned. The strength and weakness of foundations is their agility and decisiveness: when they decide to act, they already have the money in hand to make things happen. But they also can be capricious in their decisions, leaving educational programs on a whim and seemingly oblivious of the competition they have spawned between institutions."[37]

---

33. Herring, "Educating Rabbis," Para. 9.
34. Sales, *Philanthropic Lessons*, 2.
35. Sales, *Philanthropic Lessons*, 2.
36. Wertheimer, "Future," Para. 27.
37. Wertheimer, "Future," Para. 27.

Hal Harvey, in "Why I Regret Pushing Strategic Philanthropy," goes further: "A major challenge for strategic philanthropy is that it can create delusions of omniscience in many program officers. Instead of reviewing grant proposals, querying experts, synthesizing ideas, and respecting those with years in the field, many program directors and officers become auteurs: They begin to see themselves as the origin of intelligence as well as the arbiters of money."[38] He insists that "The grant-making business already starts with a deep imbalance of power, with one party wielding the decision-making authority and the other more or less on bended knee. Add the presumption of strategy, and in no time, grant seekers become whipsawed approval-seekers and grant makers become demigods — with all the theocratic arbitrariness that term implies."[39] "When you find good nonprofit leaders or groups, give them the benefit of the doubt," he advises. "Go to first principles: You are lucky that the groups and leaders are already strong. A grant maker's job is to support those institutions and leaders. Write the check and get out of the way."[40] Harvey explained the fundamental principle of good strategic philanthropy: "Respect the strategic insights of others and learn to keep a light hand on the process and reporting buttons. Good intentions badly applied can crush the best leaders and the best groups. By all means, be strategic in building foundation programs, but don't confuse that work with either program omniscience or suffocating process. You will kill what you are trying to create."[41]

The fact is that national educational organizations like RAVSAK, absent a high dues or fee-for-service structure, will not be supported by local organizations. Shari L Edelstein, Marcella Kanfer Rolnick, and Yossi Prager spelled out the problem in an article in *eJewish Philanthropy*. "As a practical matter, national philanthropists have largely assumed the burden of supporting national 'field-building' organizations and often encounter little willingness from local funders to support these cross-community organizations," they wrote. "We see this as short-sighted. Powerful 'field builders' share information and best practices on a wide variety of developments and trends in their respective fields; they offer a global perspective on shared issues, and develop centrally provided programs that are by their nature more cost-effective. The added value of these organizations can influence

---

38. Harvey, "Why," Para. 2.
39. Harvey, "Why," Para. 3.
40. Harvey, "Why," Para. 22.
41. Harvey, "Why," Para. 24.

national directions and support local efforts for change. And it is increasingly clear that the national philanthropists do not have adequate capital to carry these organizations alone."[42]

Yet despite offering a series of recommendations for furthering collaboration between national organizations and local funders, there seems to have been little positive response or reaction to their position. Ironically, ten months into a funding collaboration between the Jim Joseph Foundation and fourteen local foundations and federations, the first conclusion reached was "While each local funder in this collaborative shares common goals and challenges, each one has different resources, different approaches to decision making, different strengths and different timelines. We must listen to every partner's needs individually and respond in a customized way, even though that means less uniformity across the cohort."[43] This need for customization and individualization seems to have surprised the Jim Joseph Foundation, despite the fact that it began with the assertion that "Every community is unique, with its own culture and constellation of leaders, institutions, and existing programs. While a national funder can bring valuable resources, expertise and perspective, local funders are best positioned to determine which new experiments will work best in their communities and to choose which partners are most appropriate to implement those experiments. These are especially critical decisions if the goal is long-term systemic change."[44]

Felix Salmon wrote a hard-hitting article in 2012 entitled "Philanthropy: You're doing it wrong." He listed ten errors common to wealthy philanthropists that seriously undermine those who receive their gifts. One of the failings is encouraging "mission creep." "If an organization is doing a good job at fulfilling its mission, you give it another task to fulfill which is not part of its mission. Instead of funding and enriching infrastructure, funding is attached to new programming and new initiatives which engage the funders' interests." Instead of living up to core values and enhancing core operations, the fundee's staff now finds itself "under constant pressure to move away from their core mission and towards where the money is."[45]

Another example of philanthropic intervention that is more detrimental than beneficial is in the area of funding collaboration efforts. David

---

42. Edelstein, Rolnick and Prager, "Supporting," Para 3.
43. Miller, "New Experiment," Para. 13.
44. Miller, "New Experiment," Para. 5.
45. Salmon, "Philanthropy," Para. 18.

LaPiana, in his 2001 monograph *Real Collaboration: A Guide for Grantmakers,* offers a sobering observation. "Funders cannot create Real Collaboration. They can only help to enhance it. In most instances, a 'grant for collaboration' will not seed or create a partnership where none existed before unless the motivation to create a partnership is present and strong."[46] Other points that LaPiana makes are that real collaboration is voluntary. "Nonprofit leaders should come together because they perceive potential synergies and benefits for their constituencies, not because a funder 'encouraged' them to do so, and least of all because a grant may be available," and that "it cannot begin, be nurtured, and mature within the limited timeframe and high pressure environment created by most funder-sponsored Requests for Proposals."[47]

Making systemic change is extremely difficult. It is an expensive, labor-intensive, conflict-laden, and most of all time-consuming process. The major foundations and mega-donors in the Jewish education world—AVI CHAI, the Jim Joseph Foundation, Sheldon Adelson, Edgar Bronfman, Bernie Marcus, Lynn Schusterman, and Michael Steinhardt—have been generous with their dollars but perhaps less than wise with their spending. They have expected miracles to occur just because they opened their wallets. In this regard, the AVI CHAI Foundation board deserves credit for not shirking its responsibility for self-assessment. Joel Fleishman's *First Annual Report to The AVI CHAI Foundation on the Progress of its Decision to Spend Down,* published in 2010, was an uncompromising and at times brutally honest assessment of the shortcomings in the foundation's philanthropic endeavors: "Perhaps the primary problem which complicates AVI CHAI's efforts to enable its grantees, even the ones of most importance to it, to cope successfully with their fund-raising needs after the lights go out at AVI CHAI is what seems to me to have been a long-prevailing 'go-it-alone' culture which AVI CHAI acknowledges but now recognizes to have shortcomings. Several of those I interviewed, both staff and Trustees, often observed that other philanthropies had not seemed to be interested in joining in AVI CHAI initiatives in the past, as well as since the spend-down was announced. But they also said that, in truth, no serious, sustained efforts had been made to seek such involvement."[48]

---

46. LaPiana, *Real Collaboration,* 6.
47. LaPiana, *Real Collaboration,* 5.
48. Fleishman, *First Annual Report,* 17.

Inadequate or misguided philanthropy is as detrimental as no philanthropy. It raises hopes and expectations, but without financial support adequate to fulfill and sustain them in the long-term, it only leads to the creation of bubbles—glistening and uplifting at first, but ultimately fated to burst.

Day School: Why do Jewish parents overwhelmingly opt for public school?

American Jewry has always wrestled with the question, Are we Jewish Americans or American Jews? The majority of those who emigrated to America, as well as the majority of those born in America, subscribe firmly to the belief that the American public school system was the nation's most important mechanism for turning Lady Liberty's "huddled masses" into productive, financially secure, democracy-loving citizens of the United States of America. Jews, native-born or foreign-born, are no exception. Having come to America at the bottom, and having risen quite spectacularly to the top, the majority of American Jews today are fully cognizant and appreciative of the role of the nation's public school system in providing them access to the very highest spheres of economic, public, social, and cultural life.

For most of the immigrants who came to the United States before the Holocaust, Americanization was the goal, without reservation. They cast Judaism aside, it is rumored, with the *tefillin* they threw overboard on their journeys across the sea. Though some minimal Jewish education was provided for some, for most it was of little import compared to the overweening value of the integration offered through the American public school system. In contrast to other religious and ethnic minority groups in the United States, Jews never looked to the public schools for the transmission of their own culture. Rather, eager to gain entry into the social and economic life of their new homeland, they considered public education the means to such ends for their children.

Jews held that religious instruction was the province of the Jewish community itself and were very comfortable with the American doctrine of separation of church and state. They also rejected the Catholic parochial school model because they did not want their children isolated from the peers with whom they were destined to spend their lives as American citizens. For the majority of the immigrants, Jewish education was an anachronism which had no place in the new world.

Challenges of the Jewish Community Day School

For many twenty-first century Jewish parents, this sentiment is as strong as ever. They see themselves as Americans first, Jews second . . . or perhaps third or fourth or fifth or not at all. Judaism is an option, a choice—one of many identities they can assume, but not their primary identity. One of the fundamental issues confronting Jewish day schools in the United States today is the disparity between the goals of day school educators and the leanings of the majority of the Jewish population for whose children such education is intended. American Jews join synagogues and send their children to Hebrew school because they want to identify as Jews, but only to a limited extent. The perfect solution, for the vast majority of Jewish parents, is the supplementary school, meeting one or two days a week after "real" school and on Sunday mornings. The benefit of this arrangement is that "neither synagogue membership nor school attendance dictate behavior that conflicts with what they perceive as the American way of life," wrote Walter Ackerman. "While parents often speak of the school as the guarantor of Judaism, they are rarely prepared to accept the implication of this position. They shy away from the recognition of Judaism as a code of behavior central to self-definition. The discrepancy between the desire for Jewish identification as such and the unwillingness to accept Judaism as formative factor has led one perceptive observer to describe involvement in Jewish education as an exercise in self-deception."[49]

For most American Jews, Jewish education was something received (and mostly detested) after public school hours, a few afternoons a week, and was intended "to do little more than prepare them for a bar or bat mitzvah ceremony, to say the mourner's Kaddish and to marry another Jew."[50] Day schools, in the view of these parents, were the creations of Orthodox Jews, who, from the outset, were accused of "parochialism, ghetto thinking and the worst sin of all—un-American behavior."[51] As a result, less than six percent of the non-Orthodox Jewish student population attends a Jewish school in the United States, writes Abraham Edelstein, noting "no other Western country with a sizable Jewish population even approaches such low rates of Jewish day school attendance."[52] He bemoans this fact, saying that "there is significant evidence that day schools are a strong vehicle in promoting Jewish continuity for the non-Orthodox. Such Jews are less

---

49. Ackerman, "Strangers," 76.
50. Pomson, "Jewish Schools," 5.
51. Ackerman, "Strangers," 16.
52. Edelstein, "Crisis," Para 1.

likely to inter-date, more likely to be Jewishly involved, and more likely to provide tomorrow's Jewish leadership. (40% of today's young Jewish leaders attended Jewish day schools.) Even amongst the non-Orthodox," Edelstein writes, "they have much lower rates of intermarriage and higher rates of joining communities and studying Torah. Parents with limited Jewish background are often the ones who grow the most through the Jewish content their children receive. No alternative model can do this. Sunday School has been shown to be ineffective in preventing intermarriage and may even do the opposite."[53]

This is a new Jewish population: comfortable in their American identity, affluent, technologically savvy, and upwardly mobile. "Values, ideologies and identities forged under conditions of deprivation and discrimination in Europe and the immigrant ghettos of America now exist within a different context," writes historian Edward Shapiro, adding that "As the disabilities of being Jewish lessened, the external pressures on Jews to identify in any significant way as Jews and to associate with the Jewish community also weakened."[54] Jewish baby boomers had a vastly different psyche from that of the generation of Jews who built the Jewish organizational structures that existed throughout the twentieth century. The post-war generation, Rabbi Sid Schwarz wrote in a June 6, 2002 article in the *Washington Jewish Week*, "does not respond viscerally to appeals based on the Holocaust or the State of Israel; they do not defer automatically to religious or communal authority figures; they do not derive their sense of place in American society primarily based on their Jewish connections." The same can be said of their offspring, in spades.

Twenty-first century parents are not convinced by experts or statistics. Leaving aside those whose reasons for enrolling in a day school are primarily religious, most Jewish parents have bypassed ethnic identification, dissatisfaction with public school, desire for small classes, and academics as their primary motives for enrolling their children in a Jewish school, particularly since their choice of where to live is so significantly based on the quality of its public school system. While those factors carry weight, what matters most today to parents are the opinions of their peers. If others in their cohort are delighted with the education their children are receiving in a Jewish day school, and say this prominently and frequently on social media and in social settings, it carries more weight than anything pundits

---

53. Edelstein, "Crisis," Para 1.
54. Shapiro, *Time*, xv.

or experts say. And unfortunately, those who are dissatisfied are more likely to post than those who are happy. Praising one's child's Jewish school calls attention to one's Jewishness, something many are reluctant to do. Even Jewish parents who are disposed to day schools are often ambivalent about them.

Network: Can the affinity, accord, and mutual understanding that bound together the heads of school and lay leaders of community day schools since the inception of JCDSN/RAVSAK be maintained in the face of the current divisions within the Jewish world?

Jewish community day schools are *sui generis*. Alike in so many ways, each is also unique, without a predetermined framework of conformity to a set of norms, no common history, ideology, methodology, or design. RAVSAK developed from the bottom up, not the top down. Community day school leaders sought out others with similar missions, goals, challenges, and issues so that they could compare, commiserate, cooperate and support one another in the absence of a larger framework. One of the major benefits of getting together, especially for smaller schools, was that it eliminated the need for each to reinvent the Jewish educational wheel in their local context. The Jewish community day school network succeeded in building collaboration and cooperation because it was a grass-roots organization at its inception and its primary focus was always on the leadership and needs of community day schools. Since its very beginning, it was an organization that did not seek to impose its views on others but to respect and support the values of like-minded institutions and help them to further their mission.

The twenty-first century only enhanced the role of RAVSAK, facilitating communication and networking through the internet, webinars, *reshetot,* and social media. Its leadership, both professional and lay, came from the community day school world. Because RAVSAK was non-denominational it was able to avoid the sharpness of rhetoric and unwillingness to seek common ground that the American Jewish Committee saw as characterizing relations between Orthodox and non-Orthodox movements. According to the AJC, "Symbolic of the collapse of dialogue was the demise of the Synagogue Council of America in 1994, the sole body that had, at least nominally, collectively represented all the Jewish religious movements."[55]

The American Jewish community does not need to add internecine warfare to its list of challenges. For one thing, as Yitz Greenberg points out,

---

55. American Jewish Committee, *Synagogue Council,* Para. 13.

"The ultra Orthodox renaissance of recent decades is of little utility for the rest of American Jewry in its struggle to achieve integration without assimilation. The Charedi solution—adopted by the co-opted centrist Orthodox camp—is to work out some geographic, cultural or ethical shelter that permits its own culture to flourish. But it cannot much help the 90 percent of American Jews who are committed to full integration and maintaining a vibrant Jewish identity inside the general culture. The continuing second-class status for women, the delegitimization of alternative movements, the exclusion of minorities, the use of monopoly and political force to impose observance on others symbolic of the collapse of dialogue was the demise of the Synagogue Council of America in 1994, the sole body that had, at least nominally, collectively represented all the Jewish religious movements—all weaken the pull of Jewish identity and culture in the eyes of more integrated Jews. These values turn them off religiously, which weakens their ability to resist assimilation."[56]

While turf battles may absorb the attention of those who are engaged in the conflict, for the vast majority of American Jews, the response is simply, "A plague on both your houses." As author Shulem Deen pointedly observes, "For centuries, nearly every Jewish male child could recite at least the beginning of the first passage of Talmud, 'From when do we recite the Shema in the evening?' Today, many of us don't care about that prayer. Jews in the twenty-first century are experiencing what is by all accounts a shift unseen since the destruction of the Second Temple. The primacy of the rabbinic paradigm—creed, practice and synagogue; the tripartite nature of traditional Judaism—is no longer relevant to many of us."[57]

A network, by definition, is a collection of units connected to one another for the purpose of sharing. Time and again, what heads of Jewish community day schools and their lay leadership valued about their network was that it allowed them to connect with colleagues who were dealing with the same issues and challenges in similarly-purposed institutions. While all schools have something to learn from one another, schools dealing with such issues as gender identification, non-traditional families, and multiple *minyanim*, gain little from schools in which these matters are not on the agenda. Truly meaningful conversations about these topics can only be held in a supportive atmosphere of mutual respect and understanding; they cannot be homogenized or removed from consideration because they are

---

56. Yitz Greenberg, "Can Modern Orthodoxy," Para. 32.
57. Deen, "Why Talmud," Para. 9.

anathema to some. Saul Wachs focused on this point. He wrote that even a great leader like Rabbi Jonathan Sacks has a very different attitude toward diversity within the Jewish community than do others. In Sacks' view, wrote Wachs, "Something cannot be true and untrue at the same time, and so the claim of Orthodoxy that the Torah is the unmediated word of God is either true or not true, and if it is true, then those Jews who interpret revelation differently are in error."[58] Those who define and maintain structures and walls between groups stand in opposition to the openness and pluralism that lies at the heart of a network.

---

58. Wachs, "Devar Torah," Para. 16.

8

Responses to the Challenges

Bavarian born Abraham Joseph Rice (1802 to 1862) was the first ordained rabbi to emigrate from Europe to America, arriving in Baltimore in 1840. Speaking no English and angered by the lack of religious observance among his congregants, he soon became disillusioned with the new land. After nine years of frustration, he left his congregation and opened a dry goods store.[1]

NO JEWISH EDUCATIONAL LEADER wants to follow the sorrowful path of Rabbi Rice into the retail business. The challenges of Jewish education in the twenty-first century can—and must—be met in meaningful ways that respond to the demographic, cultural, societal, and technological realities of the age.

By the end of the first decade of the twenty-first century, sociologist Alex Pomson reported that more Jewish children attended Jewish day schools than at any other time in history. He estimated a worldwide enrollment of 1.4 million, three quarters in Israel, 225,000 in North America, and approximately 125,000 more "scattered across the globe in every continent other than Antarctica."[2] Pomson also noted that the growth in numbers was accompanied by a growth in religious diversity. Whereas in the twentieth century most of those enrolled in day schools came from Orthodox

---

1. Pluralism Project, "Judaism in America," Para. 24.
2. Pomson, "Jewish Schools," 1.

homes, at the beginning of the new millennium a significant portion of the growth in enrollment consisted of non-Orthodox children. The implications of this phenomenon for Jewish leaders in the twenty-first century are profound. Pomson points out that until as recently as the 1980s, "Parents whose children attended a school were, typically, synagogue members and residents of Jewish neighborhoods who had themselves received a relatively intensive Jewish education. With few exceptions, these parents were Jewish from birth, Orthodox in denominational orientation, and married to other Jews: people for whom paying for all day Jewish school for their children constituted the ultimate expression of an already intensely engaged Jewish identity."[3]

The Jewish context of the twenty-first century is considerably different. Jewish day schools reflect the increasing religious variety of contemporary Jewish families, including those that are conversionary, interfaith, same sex, unaffiliated, doubting, wondering, and searching. Many of these families lack Jewish education and depend on the schools to help them find a place in Judaism. "The community day school has become the central focus of Jewish life in many communities with the obligation and privilege or perpetuating Jewish life and learning in that place," wrote Cooki Levy, former head of the Akiva School in Montreal, in a private correspondence with the author. "For the non-orthodox, in many communities, the school has taken the place of the synagogue as the institution with which Jews affiliate. Parents who have little or no Jewish knowledge or education of their own are looking to connect for their children. They choose the school over the synagogue, and that gives the schools the responsibility to serve the entire family in their search for Jewish meaning and for a way to live some kind of Jewish life. Providing Jewish programming and experiences is a major part of the school's role, and, in fact, deepens and expands the Judaic content of the school."

It is vitally important to recognize the implications of these shifts. As Jonathan Woocher wrote, "We live now in a different time, a time of hybrid identities and multiple communities. For most younger American Jews, the issue is not whether or not to be Jewish—they are Jewish, and their Jewishness is in no sense a burden or a barrier. But with many identities intermingling in their self-definition and with many communities available within which to pursue the things they value in life, the significance of their Jewishness is very much up for grabs. The new question that Jewish

---

3. Pomson, "Jewish Schools," 5.

education must answer is not about group preservation, but about personal meaning."[4] Twenty-first century Jews, Woocher wrote, seek for their lives the same things others seek: "A modicum of security amidst turmoil, a sense that their lives matter, satisfying connections with others, the feeling of being in control, pride in accomplishment." The big question, he asserts, is, "Will their Jewishness contribute substantially to any of this? Can Judaism, Jewish Community, Israel, the Jewish people, Jewish culture, and Jewish learning be a powerful resource for them as they seek to construct meaningful, fulfilling, purposeful, and responsible lives?"[5]

Jewish education needs to adjust to its time and place. As Jonathan Krasner says, "The Eurocentric narrative arc, with its dramatic story of emancipation, destruction and Zionist rebirth, is undeniably compelling and consequential. But it is also increasingly distant from and incongruous with the lived experience of Jewish young people in North America today. Far from a failure, citizenship and integration has yielded an unprecedented degree of acceptance, security and prosperity for Jews in the United States and Canada. Concurrently, the American Jewish community has become increasingly ethnically and racially diverse, with fewer Jewish young people tracing their lineage (exclusively) to central and Eastern Europe."[6] Tsvi Bisk and Moshe Dror make the point even more forcefully, declaring that it is time to reject the notion that the history of the Jews is only one of suffering and persecution. "Many peoples have suffered terribly in human history, the Jews included," they write, "but neither human history nor Jewish history is simply the story of suffering . . . Jewish hand-wringing is a hazard to our well-being. How can it not alienate increasing numbers of young Jews? What mentally healthy person wants to be part of a culture that is dedicated to never-ending mourning, let alone devote his or her life to that culture?"[7]

Judaism and Jewish education need to be reformulated for those twenty-first century Jewish families who are not turning their backs on modernity but nonetheless want something appropriate to the time and place they inhabit. Following are some proposals to address the issues of Jewish education in America, in the context of the Jewish community day school movement and in direct correlation with the problems identified in preceding chapters.

4. Woocher, "Jewish Education," 206.
5. Woocher, "Jewish Education," 206.
6. Krasner, "Between," Para. 3.
7. Bisk and Dror, "Jewish Community," Para. 15.

Responses to the Challenges

Stop Trying To Define/Confine/Refine Who Is Jewish

The pluralistic vision of Horace Kallen and Mordecai M. Kaplan has been fulfilled in contemporary America. Cultural pluralism has come to define the nation. Adherents or descendants of any ethnic or religious tradition can now retain their distinctiveness while participating in an American society composed of many different ethnic and religious groups. American Jews are now free to assimilate or to exist voluntarily as a separate community. But there are nightmarish aspects to the Kallen/Kaplan dream. At a time of political unrest, xenophobia, bigotry, misogyny, and racism are on the rise, as is evidenced by the appalling low level of the political discourse during and following the 2016 presidential campaign, the ugliness of what passes for commentary on social media, and the hatreds finding expression after the 2016 election. Furthermore, the pace of evolution of Jewish Americans from American Jews to just plain "Americans whose families used to be Jewish" is accelerating. The American Jewish community as it existed in the past is in trouble today. Demographically, the population is in decline, not only in absolute terms but relative to the country as a whole. Jack Wertheimer lists the mounting evidence that supports this assertion: "Synagogue membership has dropped by nearly one-third over the past half century; Jewish community centers are relying ever more heavily on non-Jewish members, while others are folding because of decreasing membership; the numbers of donors to federations of Jewish philanthropy have plummeted by some 45 percent over the past thirty years."[8]

Rabbi Rami Shapiro lamented, "What troubles the rabbis I've been talking with is that after decades of trying to create a vibrant and intrinsically compelling Judaism we find that most Jews just don't care. While 69% of American Jews are proud to be Jews, 22% have abandoned Judaism and only 15% identify Judaism as essential to being Jewish. We are rabbis, not Jewish Community Center directors. We uphold Judaism the religion. Not only have we failed to bring more Jews in, we may be witnessing the exodus the few Jews we have left."[9] Rabbi Ammiel Hirsch went further, predicting in a *Huffington Post* article that the existence of so many entirely secular Jews threatened their very survival and that practically none will have Jewish descendants by the third generation. "Centuries, perhaps millennia, of Jewish life in those families will end within the next generation or two," he declared, "no matter how strongly these Jews profess their Jewish

---

8. Wertheimer, *Imagining*, viii.
9. Shapiro, "Response," Para. 1–2.

identity, or sincerely want Jewish grandchildren." Yet instead of addressing this issue, there are many whose major preoccupation seems to be defining who is "in" and who is "out" against a growing background of others whose response is "who cares?"

There are those who feel smug in asserting that Haredi Judaism is a bulwark against assimilation and that its dramatic demographic growth is proof of its success and viability in the future. Jeffrey S. Gurock, in *Orthodox Jews in America*, suggests that even amidst cultural differences in the Orthodox world, all Orthodox Jews "share the sense that their and the next generations' futures are well assured. The more triumphalist within their midst would even argue that not only had they proven that it was possible to remain true to the halacha while moving forward within an accepting society, but in fact, that their formula is the only recipe for future Jewish survival in America. Some go so far as to predict that by the end of the twenty-first century, Orthodoxy's committed cohorts might well be the only Jews left in the United States."[10]

But the reality on the ground is different and the reason is primarily economic. Seth Kaplan and Naftuli Moster decry the fact that the American Jewish community, "well known for its educational achievements, philanthropy and investments in communal organizations and services . . . has mysteriously allowed a significant portion of its own community to grow up undereducated, without the skills to earn a basic living."[11] They write that "The marked growth of a Haredi community in which students lack basic work skills will mean that within about two generations, a significant portion of the Jewish population—maybe even a third or more—will be unable to earn a decent living, unable to contribute financially or practically to Jewish institutions, and unable to partake in American life as ordinary citizens. The poverty rate will be higher than any time since the middle of the 20th century."[12]

"Torah study has become for Haredim a weapon in the war against the corrupting influences of life outside the Haredi cultural enclaves,"[13] writes Samuel Heilman. "Full-time study in a yeshiva by a man who would otherwise be a breadwinner or having a large family despite a low income [is seen] as evidence of the highly valued *mesirat nefesh*, religious sacrifice

---

10. Gurock, *Orthodox*, 246.
11. Kaplan and Moster, "Why," Para. 17.
12. Kaplan and Moster, "Why," Para. 17.
13. Heilman, *Sliding*, 143.

and dedication."[14] But the social and economic costs of removing over half of all young men from gainful employment keep increasing. Heilman explains: "Parents who have four children, each of whom is married and in the marriage of each of which the breadwinner is studying in a *kollel* and the wife has borne four to seven children, find themselves having to support, partially or entirely, up to thirty-two people in addition to themselves. That is an extraordinary financial burden."[15] The result is tremendous debt; 63 percent of Hasidic Jewish families in New York City are poor. In April 2016, *The New York Times* reported that of America's 3,700 villages, towns, or cities with more than 10,000 people, none had a higher proportion of its population living in poverty than Kiryas Joel, the Satmar enclave in New York State. "Haredi society lives in anticipation of the time in the not-too-distant when today's generation of *avrechim* must start marrying off its children,"[16] writes Tamar El-Or. But "unlike the previous generation, which had some resources from which to provide financial assistance to its children, the current generation has nothing. It also has a larger number of children than its parents' generation did, and the standard of living is higher. In preparation for this approaching crisis, the public discourse has been enlisted in the condemnation of prosperity and the glorification of living simply. Haredi society's unique organization as a learning society, made possible by prosperity, may be destroyed by the very thing that created it."

The reality is that in the twenty-first century it is impossible to live in a ghetto, even a self-imposed ghetto. Technology, which now dominates life, is making inroads whether we like it or not. From Shabbes elevators to keyless hotel entry to kosher cell phones, technology is infiltrating observant life. Chabad has mastered the web and social media; young *Haredim* have begun to observe *hetzi Shabbat*, returning to their phones midway through the day in order to stay connected with their peers. Schools to train Haredi men to do computer programming are being created in the United States and in Israel. And while Orthodox schools may try their hardest, may refuse entrance to a student whose family owns a television and may ban smartphones, their ability to staunch the effects of contemporary society in the swift-moving, rapidly changing world of today is more limited than ever before.

14. Heilman, *Sliding*, 143.
15. Heilman, *Sliding*, 146.
16. Tamar El-Or, *Educated*, 191.

That does not mean that things are better for the more liberal denominations. "Once considered the wave of the future and a bridge to the non-Orthodox movements, no sector is as beleaguered today as are the Modern Orthodox,"[17] wrote Steven Bayme. "As the influence of *roshei yeshiva*—one of whom went so far as to equate the Modern Orthodox of today with Amalek—has increased, moderate voices within Orthodoxy have receded. While Modern Orthodoxy currently acknowledges the commonality that Jews share in terms of their history, origins and values, regardless of religious orientation, as they face increasing pressure from the right to differentiate themselves from both less-observant and other-observant Jews and non-Jews, they will increasingly raise barriers between the members of the Jewish people." Yeshiva University, the flagship and standard bearer of Modern Orthodoxy is in grave financial and existential distress. A 2016 article in the *Forward* asked, "Will the institution continue its two-decade project of transforming into a major research university? Or have the school's leaders settled on return to the college's religious roots as the only way to save the institution at the heart of Modern Orthodoxy?"[18] Its new president is tasked with dealing with major fiscal challenges, including losses of approximately $85 million for each of the last two years, a faculty that has had no salary increases since 2008, and a downgrading of the university's credit rating. At the same time, he must address what has been characterized as the intramural ideological wars within Modern Orthodoxy.

The Conservative movement has its own deep-seated challenges. While 43 percent of American Jews affiliated as Conservative Jews in 1990, just 18 percent do so twenty-five years later. This is causing much soul-searching in the Conservative movement. "There isn't a single demographic that is encouraging for the future of Conservative Judaism. Not one,"[19] wrote Edward S. Shapiro in an article entitled "*The Crisis of Conservative Judaism*," quoting Rabbi Edward Feinstein. Shapiro noted that "the National Jewish Population Survey of 2000–01 reported that the percentage of congregationally affiliated American Jews who identified with Conservative Judaism had declined from 43 percent to 33 percent during the 1990s, and this decline, as the 2011 survey of Jews in the New York City area indicated, has continued during the past decade."[20] Reform Judaism

---

17. Bayme, *Arguments*, 343.
18. Nathan-Kazis, "New President," Para. 3.
19. Shapiro, "Crisis," Para 4.
20. Shapiro, "Crisis," Para. 4.

Responses to the Challenges

fares little better. As Marty Linsky wrote, "The challenges facing Reform Judaism may feel unique, but they reflect larger forces sweeping through society. In the Jewish world, the Reform Movement faces issues that are all too familiar: the high rate of intermarriage, the pull of other Movements, including Orthodoxy and Chabad; and the disinclination of Jewish millennials, like their non-Jewish peers, to identify with institutions of any kind, particularly the traditional ones that were part of their childhood. In the broader community, we are in the midst of a period unlike any before in our lifetimes. Change—and rapid change, at that—is a constant, with all the consequences attendant to it. The future is uncertain and unpredictable, and decisions must be made with inadequate information."[21]

In an era where every Jewish population is threatened by the challenges of modernity, including assimilation, renascent anti-Semitism, and intermarriage, it might be logical to think that a "circle the wagons" mentality would take hold, and that leaders of all segments of the Jewish community would try to unite in an effort to stabilize the situation if not reverse its course. Nothing could be further from the truth. The divisions are simply too wide. The denominations of Judaism within American society are struggling hard to redefine themselves and to avoid going out of business altogether. The divide between traditionalists and modernists within the Orthodox community widens yearly and the Orthodox—be they Haredi or Modern—are ever less accepting of their more liberal co-religionists.

While the denominations spend time and energy jockeying for position as the largest (Reform), most successful (Modern Orthodox), most prolific (Haredi,) and most centrist (Conservative) segments of American Judaism, the Jewish population has moved on to post-denominationalism. Sociologist Steven M. Cohen identified the trend more than a decade ago: "In the last few years, two trends, distinctive but often conflated, have come to characterize the denominational identity patterns of American Jews. One we may call 'non-denominationalism,' in which Jews decline to see themselves as aligned with Orthodoxy, Conservatism, Reform, or Reconstructionism (the major denominational choices available to American Jews). On social surveys, when asked for their denominational identity, they answer, or are classified as, 'Just Jewish,' 'Secular' or 'Something else Jewish.' In contrast, we have a relatively new phenomenon that embraces only a very small number of Jews, many of whom, it seems, are in their twenties and thirties. This contrasting trend we may call 'post-denominationalism.'

---

21. Linsky, "Future," Para. 1–3.

It refers to committed Jews, congregations and educational institutions that abjure a conventional denominational label for one reason or another. As individuals, they experience ideological and stylistic differences with the available denominational options. As institutions, their leaders seek to appeal to a multi-denominational constituency, be it of congregants, students or donors."[22]

But a more fundamental question is: *What does it matter?* The fact is that denominationalism belongs to twentieth century America. Instead of spending time defining what "Jewish" is, what gender a rabbi can be, and whose conversion is legitimate, it would be better to devote effort and expenditures on ensuring that "Jewish" will be, lest the Jewish community find itself, as Rabbi Clifford Librach wrote, "on the road to religious oblivion."[23]

Community schools do not need nor do they seek to define who or what is Jewish. "While some communities are based on sameness and aspirations of homogeneity," writes Rabbi Mitchel Malkus, "pluralistic schools and communities center around the awareness of others, multiple viewpoints, practices and beliefs, and the interdependence of all community members. Of course, there is a large degree of shared values, culture, and heritage that unites a pluralistic Jewish community. It just comes together with a deep respect for and celebration of the various ways Jews approach our common tradition and history. Pluralistic Jewish day schools cultivate environments that are open-minded, welcoming, tolerant, and diverse. At the same time, pluralistic schools teach students to understand and develop familiarity with practices and beliefs that differ from their own. Understanding what other people believe and value is a primary characteristic of pluralism. Beyond this, a pluralistic Jewish school affords students the opportunity to enrich and enhance their own identity significantly, as they respectfully confront, debate, and grapple with difference. Students gain a greater appreciation for the totality of what it means to be Jewish and the varieties of expression serious Jewish engagement takes."[24]

This does not mean, however, that all day schools are or must be alike. The Orthodox cannot change their positions; by definition they must adhere to the strict interpretations they espouse. By definition, community schools are pluralistic. The two cannot ever walk the same walk or talk the same talk. It is pointless to expect people who do not and will not speak the

---

22. Cohen, "Non-Denominational," Para. 1–2.
23. Librach, "Conservative Judaism," Para. 3.
24. Malkus, "What Defines," Para. 1–2.

same language to have a conversation and communicate in any meaningful way. The Jewish community day school movement realized the vision of those who wished for unity and equality among those branches of the Jewish family who hold each other in mutual esteem. It is vital to recognize the enormity of this accomplishment. While both Orthodox and non-Orthodox schools have similar needs, primarily involving funding, other areas of need such as professional development, teacher training, admissions, curriculum, and even governance, will inevitably flounder on the shoals of the differences between the two mindsets, which are of sufficient magnitude as to require disjunction. Sometimes, as it says in *Kohelet*, "*Tovim hashnayim min ha'echad*," two really are better than one. It is not a matter of Orthodoxy being "better" or "more" Jewish; there are just areas of disagreement that cannot be bridged. Orthodox Judaism can never accept Reform or Conservative Judaism or even Modern or Open Orthodoxy, nor can it grant equal status to women or fully accept homosexuals or transgendered people, or children of interfaith marriages. While an Orthodox school can make great strides in accommodating those with special needs, it can never be as fully open and accessible in general as is the community day school. The Modern Orthodox world still has to choose its direction in the twenty-first century. The community day school world already made its choice.

In A Transdenominational World, Support Community

"Judaism is about community," said Rabbi Michael Strassfeld to his congregation on the first day of *Rosh HaShanah* 2006, "a community that links us to the community of the Jewish people of the past—a community that also helps us link to the unfolding Jewish future but most of all a community that links us to the present. Judaism is meant to be lived in community, not alone on a mountain top, not just in family, but in community."[25]

Despite the beleaguered state in which contemporary Jewry finds itself, there is hope for a resurgence of cohesion even as the arguments and estrangements continue. "If anything, disunity has been the norm of Jewish history,"[26] noted Steven Bayme, Director of Jewish Affairs of the American Jewish Committee. In the twenty-first century, the fundamentals are unchanged, though the context is different. In today's world cameras are swallowed to survey the intestinal tract, cars drive themselves, phones take pictures, connect to the Internet, and serve as ATMs and payment terminals. This technology is appealing to all —just walk around the *kotel*

---

25. Strassfeld, "Open Society," Para. 14.
26. Bayme, *Jewish Arguments*, 343.

(Western Wall in Jerusalem) and see how many Jews wearing 18th century garb have cell phones glued to their ears. What is needed in the twenty-first century is an awareness of just how alike the constituent elements of Judaism are and how community needs can be fostered.

Jack L. Seymour and Elizabeth Caldwell explain that a faith tradition needs to be taught and its multiple means of expression need to be explored. They elucidate: "Rarely are religious communities univocal. While holding to a common set of practices, beliefs, ritual expressions, or values, each religious community embodies a range of diverse expressions as they are affected by culture, context, and public events. How a person of faith negotiates the terrain of living and contributes to the wider health and thriving of it is an essential question and task of religious education."[27] This is the role of the community day school.

Pluralism does not mean "anything goes" or the dreaded term "relativism." It merely means, again in Rabbi Strassfeld's words, that "we stop talking about the good Jews and the ones who are helping to end the Jewish people and talk about the variety of Jews. We don't judge or compare, we teach and listen to each other and respect those whose Judaism is deeply different than our own."[28] The Chabad model of positive outreach and acceptance of Jews of every level of observance and belief is worthy of emulation. *Klal Yisrael* needs to be the rallying cry of those segments of twenty-first century Jewry who choose to be full participants not only in Jewish and American life but in modern life. We need to recognize, as Steven Bayme points out, that "the common problem facing Jews lies far more in assimilation and religious indifference than in religious pluralism" and that "on the contrary, the availability of diverse models of religious expression may act as a corrective to assimilation."[29]

Bayme posits four components of true pluralism:

> *No group possesses a monopoly on religious truth. We all need to learn from one another, or, in the words of the Talmud, 'Who is a sage, one who learns from all humanity.'*

> *Different Jews will require different avenues to connect with Judaic heritage. No single formulation of Jewish expression will work for all Jews. Rather we need multiple entry points and pathways to Jewish identification.*

---

27. Seymour and Caldwell, *Preface*, xi.
28. Strassfeld, "Open Society," Para. 14.
29. Bayme, *Jewish Arguments*, 344.

Responses to the Challenges

> *Pluralism should not be involved to validate whatever Jews do. Religious relativism, indeed, mandates an 'I'm OK, you're OK' attitude in which religious truth and conviction lose all meaning. As Dr. Norman Lamm has put it eloquently "if everything is kosher, then nothing is kosher." Rather pluralism does mean the freedom to criticize one another but in an atmosphere of respect and cooperation rather than delegitimation.*
>
> *Pluralism connotes a clarion call to combat religious indifference. Its essential message means increased religiosity rather than freedom from religion.*[30]

These words resonate with the intentionality of Jewish community day schools. The Jewish community day school movement fulfills the hopes of those who wish for unity among those branches of the Jewish family that hold each other in mutual esteem, regardless of denomination. Committed to transideological Jewish education, community day schools acknowledge the validity of all major streams of Jewish thought and incorporate this principle into their curricula and ethos. This acknowledgement implies that there exist many options for the expression of Judaism. Community day schools prize, appreciate, and advocate for the value concept of *Klal Yisrael* and promote participation in Jewish community life, regardless of its ideological basis.

It is important to remember how the community day school movement started. It began because the needs of community schools could not be met by any of the categories of the various movements of Judaism then or now in existence. It began with a small group of schools that were unique and specific to their own communities and the people in them. In the words of the founders, as resonant today as when they were written:

> *The primary purpose of a Jewish communal day school is to serve the Jewish community in which it is located, by offering that community the finest Jewish education possible. It follows, therefore, that a Jewish communal day school must be responsive to, and representative of its community, excluding none of the various Jewish philosophical and ideological groups of which the community may be composed. Rather the communal school must exhort the Jewish community at large, its Klal Yisrael, to a heightened Jewish consciousness, strengthened identity, and deepened commitment, without delineating dictates of religious ideology or designating preferred religious tenets or philosophical ideal . . . The communal school must approach*

---

30. Bayme, *Jewish Arguments*, 344.

Judaism, in all aspects of Jewish practice and modes of thought, with reverence, respect and without prejudice, regardless of the specific practices of the school.

While it is incontrovertible that the Haredim have been highly successful at providing both educational and social frameworks that have resulted in demographic resurgence, it has come at the price of isolation from the mainstream of society. And while the Orthodox population is growing and may well become half of the Jewish population by the end of the twenty-first century, it cannot be the case that the other half is forgotten or ignored. "The Pew study said that the party is over; that American Jews don't care and aren't going to care," wrote RAVSAK's Marc Kramer in an unpublished article. "But the community day school is the place that bucks the tide. Community day schools are evidence that Pew is not the only lens to understand the Jewish community. Community day schools are the educational portals through which Pew Jews face the future." The growth of community day schools needs full encouragement and support.

Another critically important role of the community day school is the one it plays outside of major metropolitan areas with substantial Jewish populations. As the 2016 presidential election demonstrated, there is life outside of big cities and it must not be written off by those living in a bubble. "The Jewish day school is an anchor, community-defining institution in smaller Jewish communities,"[31] explain Mark L. Goldstein and Marilyn Forman Chandler. "Strong Jewish day schools of excellence are vital components of the infrastructure of a vibrant Jewish community. They enable communities to attract Jewish education-committed newcomers, including clergy and Jewish communal professionals. They enable families choosing a more enriching Jewish education for their children to remain in the community. They attract Jewish educators who are able to broaden a community's Jewish learning or connection to Israel. As such, their sustainability in smaller communities is a community issue requiring community collaboration. Federations and day schools should come to recognize that their respective success is inextricably linked to each other, as well as to other community-based Jewish organizations. This rising tide really does raise all ships."[32]

Community day schools are also in a unique position to address another issue, that of parents who never had a Jewish education or one that

---

31. Goldstein and Chandler, "Promoting," Para. 16.
32. Goldstein and Chandler, "Promoting," Para. 16.

left a significant impact on them, but who nonetheless want something different for their children. This is the case for most non-Orthodox parents in the twenty-first century. Ken Gordon, writing in *Kveller*, explained it thus: "A few years ago, my then-boss—a yarmulked über-Jew named Yossi Abramowitz—asked if I planned to send my kids to day school. I don't remember my response, but I can tell you what I thought: 'Dude, are you kidding?' I was a secular public-school kid, my wife was a secular public-school kid, and my children, when they were old enough, would follow pedagogical suit. We didn't pay those insanely super-high Newton, Mass. taxes for nothing."[33] Gordon went on to enroll his children in a day school and was supremely happy with the results, but his initial reaction strongly mirrored that of most non-Orthodox Jewish parents in the twenty-first century.

For many Jewish parents who had minimal or no Jewish education, all things Jewish are anxiety-provoking if not outright threatening. One's very parental status is endangered when placed in a situation in which there is little or no comprehension of its language, rituals, or purpose. How can one teach one's children what one does not know oneself? For many Jews the synagogue is an alien environment, Jewish history is the story of recurrent disasters, Israel is an enigma at best, and discomfort is the predominating emotion. Now consider the feelings of Jews by choice and interfaith families, who do not even have the familial, culinary, or cultural connections that many Jews have. It is not surprising that assimilation provides a welcome relief from the stress of being Jewish.

But to ignore or write off these parents and families or to make evermore restrictive and isolationist Orthodox education the only option available to them is to make a tremendous mistake. Community day schools open up the joy of the Jewish world to those who never experienced it as joyous, who found Hebrew school boring and a waste of time, who were turned off by learning that had no relevance to their daily lives, and no future beyond bar or bat mitzvah. It can offer new Jews and interfaith families a welcoming introduction to a new world, centered around their deep love for their children. Community day schools, with their commitment to both secular and Jewish studies, their engagement with the larger community, and their embrace of the multicultural, pluralistic reality that is America in the twenty-first century can provide a needed antidote to decades of failed Jewish education.

33. Gordon, "Seize," Para. 1.

Some have even gone so far as to suggest that day schools could supplant synagogues. Ken Gordon, the parent cited earlier, wrote another op-ed in which he suggested that "Jewish day schools could be, like synagogues themselves, for the entire Jewish community. They should be the place where people come to study, a home for everything from early childhood education to traditional day school study, b'nai mitzvah prep and adult education. Imagined this way, day schools would have a much larger base and a much greater opportunity to build lifetime relationships. Why shouldn't day schools take the lead in lifetime learning?"[34] Marc Kramer notes that "Parents may in fact be trying to connect themselves and their families with Judaism by enrolling their children in a day school, acknowledging that their children may soon know more than their parents do about the religion, about Hebrew . . . and about Jewish identity. In a sense," Kramer said, "the community Jewish day school is throwing a Jewish lifeline to those Jews who have strayed from affiliation, identification, and participation in Jewish worship and life. Whereas this phenomenon is also true of the denominational schools, Jewish community day schools reach out to the largest and fastest-growing segments of the American Jewish community: the intermarried and the unaffiliated."[35]

It seems highly unlikely that schools will supplant shuls, but in the twenty-first century, partnerships and coalitions are highly prized. There are already many cases in which schools and synagogues share space, staff, and programming and these ventures deserve to be expanded and championed. Despite longstanding division, if not outright hostility, between day schools and congregations (for reasons that are truly incomprehensible), the time has come for clerical and lay leadership of both institutions to realize that they share an interest in working together and forgetting "turf" issues. Day school attendance and synagogue membership are synergistic, not mutually exclusive. In the twenty-first century, synagogues and day schools need to reconcile whatever differences they believe separate them. Ultimately, the divisions will probably prove more apparent than real. Both *shuls* and schools seek committed, knowledgeable, practicing adherents to the Jewish faith and they represent different, non-competing paths to the same end result. Clearly there are economic factors at play, but is it truly possible that the fate of the Jewish community will be held hostage to

---

34. Gordon, "Turning," Para. 9.
35. Kramer, "Teaching," Para. 68.

budgetary considerations, with no effort made to develop creative, mutually-supportive resolutions to these economic challenges?

Rabbi Arthur M. Ruberg of Congregation Beth El in Norfolk, Virginia, guest-wrote an article in a JCDSN newsletter about "The Congregational Rabbi and the Day School." Ruberg noted that "All current studies of the American Jewish community document the increasing importance and value of Jewish day school education" but stated quite frankly that "there was a time when some rabbis viewed the day school as a threat to the synagogue and to synagogue based education" and "would focus on the day school's failings and limitations." He wrote that while "it is still true that day school alone is no guarantor of adequate religious education and commitment as some of its parents think it is," nevertheless "it should be obvious to every rabbi that the advantages of our children getting a day school education far outweigh any disadvantages. By and large the most committed and most knowledgeable parents in our congregations today choose to send their children to Hebrew day schools. It is, as they say today, a 'no-brainer' that rabbis must cultivate those students and their families." Rabbi Ruberg made some very specific suggestions of principles, programs, and priorities for rabbis to use in supporting their local day schools, including the following sage observation: "No one on the Jewish ideological spectrum is ever completely satisfied in a community day school setting. But the sense and experience of Klal Yisrael has its definite benefits. While I am a Conservative rabbi, I believe strongly that my own children's experience at the school has been enhanced and enriched by their exposure to Orthodox and Lubavitch faculty. I have heard it said also that those faculty members have had their eyes opened as well by coming into contact with committed and observant non-Orthodox students. Our school has benefited by the presence of students, faculty, and parent body representing all parts of the community. The broad spectrum is a challenge but one that is well worth the effort to manage."

As the Jewish world splinters and fractures over myriad differences of opinion about "who is a Jew," as the Orthodox world moves to the right and trumpets that its demographics will mow down the competition, the rest of the world is moving on, with Jews or without them. American society can accommodate isolationist subpopulations like the Amish; it can (at least for now) tolerate pockets of determined though impoverished Jews in places like Kiryas Joel, but the fact is that American demography is changing as significantly as Haredi demography. By 2080, the majority of Americans will no longer be white, but people of color. Before 2040, Muslims are projected to become the second-largest religious group in the United States, after Christians. The old Protestant/Catholic/Jewish triad no longer exists. American Jewry needs to find its place in this new American century and it will be a new and different place. Thoughtful voices are already beginning to be heard on the subject. Matthew Boxer, a research professor at the Cohen Center for Modern Jewish Studies at Brandeis, makes the point that "the last time American Jewry operated as a cohesive, united community may have been when a small group of Jewish refugees alighted in New Amsterdam in search of refuge from the Inquisition."[36] He does not see the lack of consensus as a negative, but instead emphasizes that "we are simultaneously strengthened and challenged by our ability as a community to accept more than one interpretation of what it means to be Jewish."[37] The voices of community point the way forward in the twenty-first century.

Times Have Changed: Make The Day School Relevant and Accessible

Arthur Hertzberg presciently forecast what has happened to the American Jewish world in the twenty-first century: "a growing weariness among some younger people at remaining Jews, marginal even under the best of circumstances," and predicted "an increasing polarization, in which part of world Jewry is quietly disappearing into various forms of secular apostasy and another part is evermore consciously affirming its Jewish character."[38] These poles were growing larger "at the expense of a rather tepid middle group, which remains very Jewish, especially in times of crisis, but is slowly evaporating. This middle group is still the majority of world Jewry."[39] Hertzberg's view was echoed by a number of other commentators. Historian Jonathan Sarna stated that "Uncertainty surrounds the question of whether twenty-first century American Jews will be able to identify a mission compelling enough for the American Jewish community to become passionate about and rally around. The great causes that once energized and invigorated American Jewry—immigrant absorption, saving European Jewry, creating and sustaining a Jewish state, rescuing Soviet, Arab, and Ethiopian Jews—all of these great missions have now been successfully completed. Today, for the first time in historical memory, no large community of persecuted Jews exists anywhere in the world. Nor

36. Boxer, "Myth," Para. 2.
37. Boxer, "Myth," Para. 5.
38. Hertzberg, "Assimilation," Para. 1
39. Hertzberg, "Assimilation," Para. 1.

Responses to the Challenges

will twenty-first century American Jews gain the kind of meaning from helping Israel, keeping alive the memory of the Holocaust, and fighting antisemitism that their twentieth century parents did; indeed, the major themes of 20th century American Jewish history—fighting antisemitism, saving world Jewry, and establishing Israel—are essentially past."[40] Sarna went on to note that while there still exist secular and universal causes that American Jews can and do embrace, "Diaspora Jews today are the poorer for not having found a well-defined, elevating [Jewish] mission to inspire them. It remains to be seen whether such a new and compelling mission can in fact be formulated."[41]

"Why would a Jew be attracted to a 'Torah' lifestyle that purports to demand estrangement from the general society, a cloistered abode, a rejection of general knowledge, an inability to function in the presence of women, a disdain for gainful employment and self-support?" queried Rabbi Steven Pruzansky, who is Orthodox. "It doesn't seem very attractive, except for one who wants to escape from the world,"[42] Liberal Rabbi Rami Shapiro declared, "The God affirmed in our liturgy is dead. The idea that the earth was created for our sake is laughable. The insistence that God loves us and will intervene on our behalf is simply sad. The notion that the people Israel is chosen and the Land of Israel is promised is seen for what it is: an Iron Age marketing campaign. Hyping Jewish jingoism to post-ethnic and post-tribal Jews and their Gentile partners is absurd. Pretending that serious Torah study consists of asking 'What does this passage mean to me today' is insulting to both Jews and Torah. And equating deep contemplative practice with clapping hands to neo-Hasidic melodies is so ridiculous that most Jews in the pews don't even bother to try."[43]

Like its enveloping larger society, the American Jewish community has become increasingly ethnically and racially diverse. Most young Jews today do not have grandparents with Eastern European accents; the Holocaust is a memorialized experience, not a lived one. As Rabbi Sid Schwarz observed in 2002, "It is time to recognize that the ethnic/survivalist agenda, which drove the Jewish communal agenda for the fifty years following the end of WWII, has run its course." He perceptively noted, "One of the reasons that the current Jewish organizational agenda does not draw many younger

---

40. Sarna, "New Millennium," 125.
41. Sarna, "New Millennium," 125.
42. Pruzansky, "Exchange," Para. 7.
43. Shapiro, "Response," Para. 5.

Jews is because its premise is the Jew as persecuted outsider. Younger Jews today are the consummate insiders, enjoying a level of success and power unimagined a generation ago. This is a generation that is ready to 'give back.'"

Jewish community day schools "got it" almost from the "get-go." As they enrolled students of color, students from nontraditional families, students with unique needs and special needs, students from many different backgrounds, community schools adapted to the new realities of the twenty-first century. They added multiple minyanim, reconfigured classrooms, and employed dynamic creative and experiential learning methodologies. They undertook programs of service learning, the alignment of study and action, and turned *tikun olam* and *tzedakah* into social service, addressing the concerns of students (and their parents) for relevant, meaningful education that went beyond texts and tests. The rest of the Jewish community didn't "get it" nearly as well. The Reform movement, the largest Jewish contingent in America, belatedly came to appreciate the role of the Jewish day school. It wasn't until 2006 that Rabbi David Ellenson, President of Hebrew Union College, wrote: "The day school provides an optimal Jewish educational setting. No other Jewish educational venue has the capacity to provide the comprehensive content and program that the day school does for both students and parents. The day school offers an education that is sustained every day, and those concerned with Jewish education must recognize the day school as a primary resource for fostering individuals who will promote future Jewish creativity and leadership."[44]

But as Rabbi Mitchel Malkus indicates, there is a need to go beyond appreciation to advocacy: "If we are going to attract the vast majority of American Jews who are not currently engaged Jewishly, we have to show the parents of our potential students why being part of our communities can be an essential component in supporting the growth of their families. Jewish day schools should seek to be the hub for Jewish education both for the families who have chosen this form of education and for the larger Jewish community . . . Jewish day schools also need to formulate their vision in a clear and concise manner, and market it together with the larger Jewish community. Many families who have not been exposed to Jewish day schools often view our learning communities as homogeneous, narrow, and parochial, when nothing could be farther from the truth. If our goal is to attract the majority of American Jews, we need to market Jewish day

---

44. Ellenson, "Future," 2.

school and its value using the best methods and practices that have been successful in other industries."[45] From the perspective of Jewish communal leadership, i.e., federations, it is vital to understand that, as Sylvia Barack Fishman explained, "Children who are enrolled in Jewish day schools participate in the creation of Jewish ethnic capital not only for themselves but for their families as well."[46]

The evidence that the success of Orthodox Judaism is attributable most strongly to their incredibly strong support of day schools seems not to cross the brain barrier into the thinking of the more liberal spheres of Jewish life. From the times of the Talmud ("A city without a school should be destroyed") until the twenty-first century, the role of the Jewish day school in keeping a community Jewishly-committed has been crystal clear. But in the twentieth and twenty-first centuries, in which the free exchange of ideas and the willingness to adapt workable solutions regardless of their source have predominated in so many other fields, the non-Orthodox Jewish educational world has stubbornly refused to acknowledge its pigheadedness in failing to promote a viable cure for the malaise of disaffiliation and disassociation in which it is mired.

Rabbi Joseph Kaminetsky, the first director of Torah Umesorah, wrote an article half a century ago entitled "A Program for the Day School Movement in the 70's and Beyond." In it, he laid out in a clear and planful manner exactly what the Orthodox movement intended—and has been able—to achieve: "We are encountering a growing degree of complacency in our day school leadership so that our enrollment has begun to drop off in many communities. To get us out of this 'enrollment rut' we need a *cheshbon hanafesh*—a critical appraisal of the directions the day school movement has taken and will take. We have to meet head-on the unprecedented change in the lifestyle taking place in the Jewish community affecting both individual and group practices, including day school programs and philosophy. Most notable of the changes is in the education and background of those heading, influencing, and participating in the day school movement. They are college educated and knowledgeable on Jewish matters. They are demanding change-but not for the sake of change alone. They are demanding change because they believe it is necessary for the survival of the day school movement. There is an ever-growing feeling that one of the objectives for day school education in the '70's and beyond must be a more

---

45. Malkus, "Can We Attract," Para. 11.
46. Fishman, *Way*, 219.

concrete and intense dedication to Torah learning. There is no doubt that this has always been one of our aims; yet some claim that it has not been emphasized enough. In our struggle to eliminate *am-har'aratzut* (uneducated Jews) and to put on the 'lights' of Torah in this country we have been successful. But to many of our critics the battle is far from over. To these critics we must project with greater intensity the idea that the day school must be basically a preparatory process to higher Jewish learning."[47]

There has never been an analogous intentional plan by the non-Orthodox Jewish community. Amy Sales has noted that American Jewish education is not effective "in meeting the challenges entailed in preparing a new generation of engaged Jews. Chief among these challenges is the difficulty of capturing the imagination of young American Jews. The world has changed since the main pieces of the infrastructure were built, and the methods and content that the system produces appear not to work in the current context. Today's youth are accustomed to diversity in all of its forms. They are well-assimilated, sophisticated, and technologically savvy. As one national educator remarked, making a map of Israel out of ice cream no longer thrills them."[48] RAVSAK's Marc Kramer pointed out that "In a technological reality that literally puts virtually everything that can be known into the palm of your hand, [the] traditional memory-based learning model is becoming less relevant."[49]

"The Jews are a wandering people, both geographically itinerant and spiritually roving. A Jew can never stay in one state of mind for too long. We debate; we change our minds; we amend."[50] These words were written by a community day school student who was proud of the fact that his pluralistic school afforded him the opportunity "to change my opinions and alter my beliefs in an environment where I can gracefully cede even my strongest certainties to new ideas."[51] In the twenty-first century, young people are attracted to things that are new, relevant, and edgy and not part of long-standing institutions. "The most fundamental problem in the context of Jewish history and social studies is the content focus of most day school classrooms," writes Jonathan Krasner in "A Day School Curriculum for twenty-first Century America." "When they aren't focused on biblical

47. Kaminetsky, "Program," 121.
48. Sales, *Philanthropic Lessons*, 1.
49. Kramer, "Literacy," para 4.
50. Wasserfall and Shevitz, "Building," 4.
51. Wasserfall and Shevitz, "Building," 4.

and Second Temple times, Jewish history and social studies curricula tend to concentrate on the Jewish experience in modern Europe and Israel."[52] While no one is suggesting that history be excised from the curriculum, there is a growing awareness that its curricular foci might need to be shifted. Philanthropist Michael Steinhardt was on this track when he called for Jewish education to tell "a Jewish story that aligns with the cutting edge of the world that we aspire to, that we know we are capable of. American Jews want a story that speaks of who they are and can be in the real world."[53]

But community is a two-way street. As community day schools strive to integrate their students into the larger world, they need the support of that world to do their work. Half a century ago, Alvin Schiff wrote: "The Jewish Day School is not without its critical problems. Chief among them are the indifference of a large segment of the American Jewish community to intensive Jewish education, the lack of a broad base of financial support, and the shortage of qualified personnel."[54] Fifty years later, nothing has changed. Non-public schools in the United States cannot operate without some stable source of funding. Tuition alone does not sustain a school and day schools do not have the endowment of selective private schools. Community support is essential and that support must be generous, open-handed, and given with pride, not reservation or resentment. The Jewish Federations of North America defines itself as "the central address of North American Jewry," and proudly asserts that it manages $16 billion in endowment assets, raises more than $900 million through its annual and emergency campaigns, and distributes more than $2 billion from its endowments and foundations. A review of the mission statements of federations from around the country reveals that their priorities have historically been synagogues, central agencies for Jewish education, JCCs, Hillels, youth movements, adult education, and summer camps. Perhaps the precarious state in which the federation movement finds itself today is attributable to the glaring question: Where's the beef?

Jewish day schools have been notably absent from the federation agenda. A 1995 study by Steven Cohen found that all forms of Jewish education, except Sunday school, were associated with higher levels of Jewish identity and that "the putative effects of day school, including non-Orthodox day

---

52. Krasner, "Between," Para. 4.
53. Steinhardt, "Emphasize," Para. 17.
54. Schiff, *Jewish Day School*, 248.

schools, are especially pronounced,"[55] but was largely ignored. A 1997 study by PEJE found that on average, local federations provided only five percent of the funds needed to educate a child in a day school. It is only recently that the federation world has noticed the impact and importance of Jewish day schools in the Jewish community of the twenty-first century. So deeply engrained is the historical rejection of the day school model that the federation movement has ignored it for decades.

The time has come for federations to take day school education off the back burner, to champion it, to support it, to see it for what it is: the guarantor of a Jewish future in the United States. The old "dual enrollment" model of public school plus Hebrew school no longer works. If American Judaism is to have a future, it must be one founded upon the advantages, both educational and social, that community day schools offer. Synagogues are no longer the most important institutions for socializing the young into the Jewish community (not enough people belong), nor are JCCs (not enough Jews belong) or Jewish camps (not enough time is spent there). The best and most effective model for imparting Jewish values, Jewish content, and Jewish connection to the young are day schools, with their full immersion in Jewish thought, history, ethics, prayer, Hebrew language, and Torah. The data are in and the results are clear: Jewish day schools make a difference; their graduates are more involved Jewishly than any other cohort; their commitment to Jewish life is stronger and their influence on the larger Jewish community is greater. It is time that the federation movement recognized and acted upon the need to sustain, support, and champion Jewish day schools. Because, as Peter Beinart wrote in a recent book review, "When American Jews were more ghettoized, Jewish continuity did not require Jewish learning. Today, when Jewish continuity is a choice, it does."[56]

The 1990 report, *A Time to Act*, spelled it out. "Community leaders have often failed to make the connection between the educational process and the knowledge that leads to commitment," it noted. "It is this lack of understanding that has prevented the top community leadership in North America from rallying to the cause of Jewish education in the same way it has to other pressing needs of the Jewish people."[57] The report went on to state that "the environment in the Jewish community is not sufficiently supportive of the massive investment required to bring about systemic change.

55. Cohen, *Impact*, 1.
56. Peter Beinart, *Review*, Para 12.
57. Commission on Jewish Education, *A Time to Act*, 40.

Responses to the Challenges

This affects the priority given to Jewish education, the status of the field of Jewish education, and the level of funding that is granted. Inevitably, insufficient community support limits the aspirations, inhibits the vision, and stifles the creativity of those involved in all aspects of Jewish education."[58]

Any push for greater community support of day school education will inevitably meet strong resistance. Federation executive John Ruskay once wrote, "The federation system does not need, nor does it seek, new purposes. The mission and broad purposes of the federation system are abiding and the needs to which it responds are prodigious. What it does need and does seek, now that the problems it faces are not imminent risks to the lives of Jews, now that we have outlived and outgrown the hostility of others as a motive for our actions, are compelling ways of articulating our rationale for Jewish life and the federation system."[59] But as Jack Wertheimer, who is certainly more knowledgeable than most about Jewish demography, said in an interview, "For much of American Jewish history, Jewish education was the province of a small sector, often toiling in near isolation. Given what we now know about powerful assimilatory trends sapping Jewish communal life, Jewish education can no longer be treated as a luxury, but as a vital necessity for the future of American Jewry. If this is properly understood, communal thinking will have to shift its priorities."[60]

It is striking that this message is so blatantly ignored even by the best thinkers of the current century. Even sociologist Steven Cohen, who has lamented the "shrinking middle" of American Jewry and is fully cognizant of the dire demographic consequences of the current situation, proposed thirteen initiatives to address the issue *not one of which is day school education*. Perhaps if federations put intensive Jewish education, through community day schools, at the top of their agendas, they would find the very rationale for their existence in the modern age, when people are rejecting the "affiliation by checkbook" of the last century. What better purpose, in the absence of imminent risks, could be addressed by federations than the enrichment of a way of Jewish life that is open to all and creates knowledgeable, open-minded, and deeply committed Jewish leaders?

The Twenty-First Century World Is a Giant Network

The "R" in RAVSAK stood for *reshet* (network). Futurists say that the unit of action in the twenty-first century is the network, not the organization.

---

58. Commission on Jewish Education, *A Time to Act*, 40.
59. Ruskay, *Historical Change*, 7.
60. Wertheimer, "Future," Para. 67.

This flies in the face of the way the Jewish educational world has operated in the past. Amy Sales highlighted the decentralization of the Jewish education system when she wrote, "Although local control of schools is an American trademark, poor connections among various elements in the field of Jewish youth education undermine the field's capacity to meet its challenges. Most notably, there are disconnections between national organizations and their local affiliates, across different types of institutions, and between the formal and informal sides of the educational field."[61]

The twenty-first century needs a different modality if Jewish education is to be meaningful and effective for the majority of Jews who are not Haredi. This is not a new problem. Decades ago, Rabbi Marc Angel identified the issues within the context of Orthodoxy: "If Orthodoxy is to meet the critical challenge of this generation, then it must reject the tendency toward narrowness and unthinking authoritarianism. It must be open, fresh, imaginative; it must give sway to the human mind and soul; it must foster diversity of thought and diversity of style—all within the boundaries of Torah and halakha. The Orthodox community must be governed by the principle of *derakheha darkhei no'am [pleasantness is the hallmark of the path of Torah]*. We must represent Torah as a sweet, pleasant and meaningful way of life. To do otherwise is to discredit Torah and to generate hatred toward Orthodoxy."[62] Angel rued the shrinking of options within Orthodoxy. "The growing narrowness in Orthodoxy is reflected by the growing narrowness in clothing styles deemed appropriate for Torah-true Jews," he wrote. "Worse, the range of legitimate intellectual and halakhic options is contracting. The forces for conformity are powerful; and one who dares not to conform will be intimidated or isolated."[63] Regrettably, Angel's appeal generated no response. If anything, the situation has worsened in the new millennium. At the same time, the need for broadening the definitions and enhancing the relationships has come ever more sharply into focus. "Relationships define and strengthen Jewish Peoplehood," wrote Rachel Gildiner. "Relationships such as those between God and Israel, parent and child, and rabbi and student are all central to our tradition. For Judaism to thrive in the future, however, Jews must focus on building relationships with other Jews. We must transcend traditional boundaries such as background, education, or level of observance, and come to deeply know one

---

61. Sales, *Philanthropic Lessons*, 3.
62. Angel, "Thoughts," Para. 11–2.
63. Angel, "Thoughts," Para 9–10.

another. Forming these strong, meaningful relationships can transform individuals and communities."[64] She concludes that, "As we increasingly become a community of communities, where Jews have many options and Jewish life takes many different forms, Jews must be able to reach across boundaries and connect with one another in meaningful ways."[65]

Those who care about the future of Judaism as a modern religious faith in the twenty-first century must address this issue forcefully and effectively. "Judaism has survived because it has been historically adaptive," write Tsvi Bisk and Moshe Dror. "From the patriarchs through the judges and kings to the prophets, throughout the 2,000-year history of rabbinical Judaism, the Jews adapted to the necessities of mostly negative external forces. However, modern global civilization has now given us the positive opportunity to exploit our adaptive gifts for our own creative growth rather than as a response to negative externals."[66] Bisk and Dror assert that "Being a Jew means to sense oneself as part of a community. Jewish identity and Jewish community are for many Jews one and the same. Significance of community is a fundamental value of Judaism. It is not an exaggeration to claim that alienation from the community is a greater cause of assimilation than one's lack of ritual observance or religious agreement. This is because being Jewish manifests itself in a sense of belonging and an active desire to attach oneself to some aspect of Jewish communal life no matter what one's level of religious observance ... Judaism might be a religion, but Jewishness is an ethnicity. Yet modernity has been eroding this sense of community for the past several centuries, and globalization now presents even greater challenges to its continuation."[67]

Community day schools can provide the fertile ground in which a community can grow. Jewish education in the twenty-first century needs to connect and network. In considering the future of the Jewish day school movement, and leaving aside Chassidic and Haredi schools, few researchers, funders, or field leaders pay sufficient attention to the details of the geographical and demographic nature of the communities in which other day schools are located. However, these factors should be of the utmost importance in considering what needs to be done to assist and maintain these schools and these communities. There is huge variability in the

64. Gildiner, "Strengthening," Para 1.
65. Gildiner, "Strengthening," Para. 6.
66. Bisk and Dror, "Jewish Community," Para. 4.
67. Bisk and Dror, "Jewish Community," Para. 2.

challenges facing day schools in a city like Boston, with ten Jewish elementary and middle schools and four Jewish high schools, and similarly-sized Nashville, which has one day school. Collaborative solutions to problems in geographically proximate schools in Florida or California are inapplicable to the five day schools in upstate New York, situated hours, miles, and hundreds of feet of snow apart from one another. Milwaukee, Chicago, and Philadelphia are listed among the twenty-five worst public school systems in the nation, according to recent surveys; recruitment in those cities is very different from recruitment in the Westchester, New York counties that are listed among the ten best school districts in America.

Buzzwords trending at the beginning of the twenty-first century are networking, collaboration and multiplicity. Classrooms are flipped; learning is personalized; choice and multiple modalities are the norm. The Jewish educational world must avail itself of these concepts, supporting schools so that they could use these new learning tools to change the educational environment. For too long funders of Jewish education just sought "new" and "bigger." They put money into new schools and into "growing" (as a verb, not an adjective) schools. They were inevitably disappointed when results were not immediate, spectacular, or sustainable. Instead of coming up with systematic, data-based, carefully-thought out strategic plans for maintaining schools in both larger and smaller Jewish communities, providing expertise tailored to the needs of specific schools, and listening to the needs of the schools as defined by their leadership instead of imposing solutions from above, funders large and small aimed their largesse at the field through well-funded agencies and then just as quickly retired from the field of battle when the war wasn't won after the opening shot. Realistically, why would a school faced with diminishing demography, significant attrition, and inadequate resources to advertise, compete, and do outreach want to grow its endowment? When a school is teetering on the brink of extinction, it's neither sensible nor realistic to do long range planning.

RAVSAK recognized from its inception that mutually beneficial cooperation and networking was the most vital part of its being. With its network of connections, and with Marc Kramer spinning the web in ever stronger and wider directions, RAVSAK was able to attract and bond day schools throughout the country in a community of relationships with a common goal and purpose: the preservation and continuation of broad-based and geographically diverse Jewish community. Not all Jewish life is lived on the United States coasts and big cities, nor should it be. Community day schools

Responses to the Challenges

are the Jewish schools most likely to be located in smaller communities throughout the country. They represent a kind of educational structure that accommodates itself to conditions on the ground, to the communities in which they are located, to the needs of real Jews of all kinds. Jewish day schools exist in a wide variety of locales. Each of these locations present different challenges and one-size-fits-all strategies for recruitment and tuition do not work. Each kind of school requires individual attention: central urban cities with large Jewish populations and a tradition of private schools and less than stellar public schools; suburban school districts with very good public school systems and high school taxes; small cities and towns with small Jewish populations, decent public schools, and competing good private schools; and schools in parts of the country with a tradition of private schooling to avoid desegregation and poor public schools.

Linking schools that have similar geographical and demographic challenges is very effective; dissimilar schools with dissimilar missions have little in common and efforts to bring them together will inevitably lead to dissention, disharmony, and disappointment. Community day schools became a movement because of their common goals, common interests, and common problems. In an epoch notable for collaboration, partnership, and synergy, schools that offer an umbrella for diverse points of view open up pathways to innovation and commitment based upon community and faith but adapting to new realities.

The twenty-first century has already made it clear that there are deep divisions within society that cannot be ignored, but rather than dwelling upon them or wasting energy in uncivil discourse, Jewish schools need to champion pluralism and focus on the core values they share. This is the direction in which younger, committed Jews are moving. In 2014 Hebrew College, a progressive, nondenominational seminary in Boston, ordained the same number of rabbis as the Jewish Theological Seminary. Josh Nathan-Kazis reported that in 2016 Hebrew College had more first-year students than all but one other non-Orthodox rabbinical seminary. "While the downward shifts in non-Orthodox enrollment aren't drastic," he wrote, "the trends are clear: the nondenominational Hebrew College is growing, while the older schools linked to a single denomination are hurting for applicants."[68] By the end of the century, the community rabbi will replace the congregational rabbi, and community schools will replace denominational schools. What is old will become new. Barriers need to come

---

68. Josh Nathan-Kazis, "Where," Para. 9.

down. Just as integrated technologies take the upper hand in our quotidian lives, so too must Jewish education embrace innovation, risk taking, and out-of-the-box thinking for its delivery systems. Networking is essential to make this happen. But networking is not just putting a group of people in the same room or a group of organizations under the same umbrella. Networking is a process of interacting and communicating with others *for mutual assistance and support*, something that can only be accomplished when there is mutual respect and acceptance. The Jewish community day school movement transcended boundaries since its inception. The value of a *Klal Yisrael* approach is even more vital in an era dominated by technology, creativity, and a desire to go global.

The handwriting is on the wall and we need to read it clearly. The twenty-first century will belong to those who embrace networking, collegiality, synergy, the common good, and *Klal Yisrael*.

9

Epilogue

It is increasingly true that diaspora Jews, if they feel Jewishly committed at all, feel that they are so by choice rather than simply by birth. Not that organic ties do not underlie the fact of their choice, but birth alone is no longer sufficient to keep Jews within the fold in an environment as highly individualistic and pluralistic as the contemporary world.

No one is more conscious of this than are the Jews themselves.

DANIEL J. ELAZAR[1]

JEWISH COMMUNITY DAY SCHOOLS rectified the mistake made by twentieth century Jewish leaders who sought accommodation without assimilation but who erred in failing to recognize that some level of insulation—not isolation—was still needed in the education of Jewish youth to make Jewish education effective. In ceding all instruction of *madda* (secular knowledge) to public schools and relegating *Torah* to a few hours of after-school and Sunday school classes, they were stacking the deck against successful Jewish learning. It is telling that the leadership of the twentieth century Jewish educational establishment that championed supplementary Jewish education (with the exception of Samson Benderly) sent their own children to day schools. And while at that time those schools were Orthodox,

---

1. Elazar, "Jewish Communal Structures," Para. 21.

were these same leaders alive today their choice would undoubtedly be the community day schools that share their commitment to pluralism and *Klal Yisrael*.

The Haredim have had tremendous success in the twenty-first century because they are not afraid to stand up for and remain faithful to their values. The rest of the Jewish community should take note. Pluralism does not mean relativism; it's not "I'm-okay-you're-okay" Judaism. Pluralism means there are many ways to be Jewish, but that it's *being Jewish* that matters. And it matters a lot. That is the philosophy that community day schools embrace. Rather than getting caught up in debating about *who* or its anagram *how*, they teach the *what* of Judaism—its history, language, Torah, prayers, laws, debates, culture, art, music, and literature.

When a house is divided against itself, three pathways present themselves: accept the breaches and try to bridge them; declare the divisions irreconcilable and accept divorcement; accept the divisions as secondary to inherently more important matters and move beyond them. The latter approach has always been that of the Jewish community day school movement. Most community day schools are small and most are elementary schools. They deal with children and their goal is to allow these children to experience the richness of their Jewish heritage and their Jewish legacy with joy and meaning. There is so much in Judaism that is positive, with messages that resonate as much in the twenty-first century as they did in preceding millennia. That is why Judaism persists, not because it is isolated and cloistered. Jonathan Woocher observed that American Jews maintain a love-hate relationship with Jewish education. On the one hand there is broad consensus that Jewish education is the bulwark against powerful tides of assimilation; on the other, there is a "perception of failure and mediocrity in the system," prompting some to question the wisdom of "pouring additional dollars into the very enterprise that has brought American Jewry to its current sorry condition."[2] But community day schools cannot be held accountable for the current state of Jewish literacy and can, in fact, point with pride to limited but still admirable success in producing literate and committed Jewish adults.

Once most Jews in America were Reform; then most Jews were Conservative; perhaps in the next generation, most American Jews will be Haredi. But pendulums swing. Even absent catastrophic world events, there is reason to believe that the present expansion of the Haredi population will

---

2. Woocher, "Foreword," xi.

Epilogue

decrease in time and the ranks of whoever is in the middle will once again swell. Still, as historian Jonathan Sarna wrote, "prophecy is a dangerous assignment for an historian of American Judaism. A cursory examination of the history of prophecies about Jews, whether in America or elsewhere, discloses that a great many of them through the years have proved wrong."[3] We cannot know whether the Jewish pendulum—swinging from the left of the *treifa* banquet, the acceptance of patrilineal descent, the ordination of women, and the acceptance of same sex marriage to the right of gender segregation, extreme *kashrut* and isolation from the modern world— is reaching the true end points of its arc.

The situation at the present time is one of flux and uncertainty. The denominational worlds are in crisis. The Modern Orthodox movement is facing the increasing stringency of the Haredim. *Tradition Renewed*, the voluminous history of the Conservative Jewish Theological Seminary of America, describes a precarious situation. "JTS is an institution in search of an ideology, and the Conservative movement atop which it sits has reached a demographic plateau. Its population pool is spilling away, first into Reform, and from there into the moral vacuum of secular America,"[4] writes Clifford Librach. He does not spare the Reform movement either, noting that "Hebrew Union College, the academic, spiritual and professional development center for Reform Judaism, is now in the early phase of reorganization. Financially the College is dependent upon a guaranteed percentage of congregational dues, but many congregations have begun to complain loudly about the burden, and the continued viability of HUC's four-campus structure (Cincinnati, New York, Los Angeles, and Jerusalem) may be in serious jeopardy. Moreover, the landscape is now dotted with other institutions producing non-Orthodox rabbis for a Jewish public moving into a post-denominational phase."[5]

In the Haredi world, troubles loom even as the population swells. Surveys from both Israel and the United States show that while Haredim will continue to increase as a percentage of the Jewish population due to high fertility rates, their growth will be tempered by large numbers of religious Jews becoming secular. Moreover, as Rabban Gamliel warned In *Pirkei Avot* (2:2), "All Torah that is not accompanied by work will eventually be negated and lead to sin." The marked growth of a Haredi community in which men

---

3. Sarna, "American Jews," 1.
4. Librach, "Conservative Judaism," Para. 33.
5. Librach, "Conservative Judaism," Para. 34.

and women lack basic work skills means that within two generations, a significant portion of the Jewish population—maybe even a third or more—will be unable to earn a decent living, unable to contribute financially or practically to Jewish institutions, and unable to partake in American life as ordinary citizens. This situation is untenable and correctives are already appearing on the horizon. There are schools in Brooklyn and Israel founded with the specific goal of teaching Haredi men and women skills that will enable them to engage in *parnasa*, earning a livelihood — and not just in small businesses and religiously-connected jobs, but in high-tech positions where salaries can support families. This entry into the digital world—now denounced in the sharpest terms—will inevitably impact Haredi lives in unorthodox—or unOrthodox—ways.

But the crisis in the denominational world pales beside the crisis in the larger Jewish community. Jewish communal leadership needs to put aside the habits of the past and focus on the future. American Judaism does not need to abandon supplementary schools or Jewish camps or adult education, but it *does* need to commit wholeheartedly to community day schools. *If nothing else, it is the one panacea that has not been tried with conviction, and it is the one remedy most likely to produce results.* What's more, as this study has attempted to demonstrate, community day schools are well suited to the twenty-first century. As Irving Greenberg wrote, "America is the most open society in human history. Everyone is exposed to varied alternative lifestyles. All people face the challenge of choice in which individuals can define their own values and existence. In such an environment, the more varieties of Jewish living the community can offer, the greater the number of people who will choose each individual variety. Each group is strengthened by the greater effectiveness of the other. Each group should be building up the other, for its own sake as well as for the greater good of clal Yisrael."[6]

Jewish families today are consumers. Chuck English described the current generation as self-focused seekers of personal gratification and fulfillment in every situation, and cravers of their own experiences. They are well-educated, have great confidence in their own abilities, see themselves as achievers, are cause-minded and goal-oriented, and focus on data and outcomes. Perhaps most uniquely, they incessantly share experiences with their online communities, and overwhelmingly value and are influenced by the opinions of those in their cohorts. "Millennials find User Generated

---

6. Greenberg, "Will there," 5.

Epilogue

Content, the views and experiences of peers, family and friends, to be more memorable and more trusted than any other content,"[7] English stated. Never has American Jewry seen a generation like this and these are the families who hold the Jewish future in their hands.

The leadership of the Jewish community—those leaders and philanthropists who can see the big picture—must recognize that today all Jews are Jews by choice. As Reuven Kimelman pointed out, "Any single dimension of Judaism cannot possibly have the range of appeal to the variety of Jews that a multi-dimensional approach will have . . . Awareness of this characteristic of modernity itself will enhance appreciation for the need of diversity in Judaism. Moreover, the fragmentation of the modern Jewish experience militates against any movement with an internally coherent ideology speaking authentically to all the different places which Jews occupy on the ideological map."[8] What we need now are schools that accommodate this multi-dimensionality and utilize it for the common good.

In the twentieth century, as sociographer Milton Himmelfarb put it, "not to be parochial Jews was our pride."[9] But the situation in the twenty-first century is very different. A certain amount of parochialism, leavened by true Jewish community spirit, is the only way to ensure a Jewish future that accommodates the complexities of this millennium. The impact of community day schools cannot be measured merely by percentage points or enrollment statistics over decades. Numbers are reflective of demographics, not measures of success, and the measurement tools used years ago are no longer flexible enough to reflect today's reality. Day schools in the non-Orthodox world serve another, even more vital purpose: safeguarding the Jewish future. While Orthodox schools strive to preserve and perpetuate the past, Jewish community schools look ahead. Rather than reject modernity, they accommodate it within a framework of Jewish education that is rich, informed, and meaningful.

Every Jewish community that has a Jewish federation should establish and fully underwrite a Jewish community day school. (Large communities, of course, should have as many day schools as demographically warranted.) But every one of the 150 communities under the Jewish Federation of North America, and as many as possible of the smaller communities under that umbrella, should have a federation-sponsored Jewish community day

---

7. English, "Maximizing," Para. 13.
8. Kimelman, "Judaism and Pluralism," 133.
9. Himmelfarb, "In the light," Para 2.

school of high quality, open to all Jewish children, and priced in such a way that no child is turned away due to inability to pay. Federations have always supported those in the community who are in need: the poor, the elderly, the sick, refugees, survivors. Now it is time for federations to support the future, a future which will be determined by the Jewish education of its Jewish children.

The American motto, *E pluribus unum*, is the natural segue into the full Americanization of Jewish education in the twenty-first century. The Jewish community day school can easily employ the same motto—One out of many—to define its pluralism, its *Klal Yisrael*. Jews share a common history, tenets, beliefs, and core values. We may differ in myriad ways, but this is nothing new. Today, even among the most rigid adherents to *halacha*, there are differences, sects, debates, even battles. But our history demonstrates that, as a community, we have survived and can survive despite these differences. That is why Jewish education matters and why the American Jewish communal leadership must take a firm and unequivocal stand to support it, not on a part-time or halfway basis, but on a full-time communal basis. The twenty-first century may be a gig economy, but Jewish education is not a gig. Jewish education is too important to be left to the whims of philanthropists and foundations. It must be the primary function of the core American Jewish leadership—the federation—to provide it. What more important role could American Jewish federations play in sustaining in supporting the Jewish community?

Most American Jews have no desire to turn the clock back and "unassimilate" their children from the American mainstream, as do the Haredim. What many of them do want, however, is a way to integrate their Judaism and their Americanism into their present and their future. Viewed through the lenses of success in the mainstream and of Jewish knowledge, engagement, and commitment, community day schools are hugely successful. They speak more clearly and persuasively to today's Jewish families than any other form of Jewish education. They fulfill a need for a contemporary and vibrant Judaism that no other schools can fill. In a post-denominational world, community day schools champion the fact that Jews need one another, regardless of affiliation. It's not a matter of either/or. It's a matter of and/and. The voices of moderation need to be heard. They have cried out in the past but have gone unheeded.

Rabbi Marc Angel was speaking in terms of Orthodoxy when he called for a faith that was "open, fresh, imaginative; [giving] sway to the human mind and soul; foster[ing] diversity of thought and diversity of style-all within the boundaries of Torah and halakha."[10] Although doubtful of the success of his vision, Angel nonetheless believed it possible "if we start to think seriously about the whole Jewish people and not just about our own immediate group."[11] The Orthodox world did not heed his words, but the community day school world did. And it is time for the federation world to listen and to act, and not just create commissions and reports.

RAVSAK had a clear vision of the direction it needed to take in the future and knew that its growth and its work must continue to be informed by its core values: *Klal Yisrael, Talmud Torah, Derech Eretz, Tzelem Elokim, Tzionut, Gemilut Chasadim, Iyun Tefilah*. Had RAVSAK and the community day school movement been allowed to continue along this trajectory, growing as schools from other movements continued to evolve into pluralistic rather than denominational institutions and had it been given sustained and sufficient philanthropic support, RAVSAK could have continued the outstanding work for which it was justly recognized. It needed a new organizational structure, a bigger staff of experienced professionals (particularly in the area of marketing and development), and a solid financial base. Partnerships and creativity were always part of the RAVSAK ethos. As a small, agile organization, not weighted down by excessive bureaucracy, RAVSAK was positioned to respond quickly and effectively to changes in the educational world. Instead of being cut off from its mission and thrust into an amalgam with which it had major and perhaps insurmountable differences, RAVSAK should have been allowed to continue moving in the direction its board rightly foresaw as necessary.

Community day schools will not go out of business because their flagship network has been cut out of the picture, but they will be weakened. The AVI CHAI Foundation knew it was taking a risk when it created Prizmah and eliminated RAVSAK. It remains to be seen if the risk will prove fatal, if community schools and their leadership will find that Prizmah meets their needs, or if they could, possibly, recreate their network in a new but equally valuable format. One cannot help but wish Prizmah: Center for Jewish Day Schools well. At the same time, one must also wonder whether Prizmah will eventually suffer from a fatally-flawed conceptual base that rejects *Klal Yisrael* and from the same attention deficit disorder that has beset other organizations created at the behest of funders seeking restructuring and

---

10. Angel, "Symposium," 8.
11. Angel, "Symposium," 8.

innovation, rather than nurturing organizations that are organic outgrowths of existing needs. Will Prizmah's funders initially and enthusiastically champion Prizmah's ideas, programming, image, branding, and data and then, after three years, lose interest when it turns out that the organization doesn't have the support, stamina, staff and financial resources to execute its operations fully and be sustainable in the long run? As Jon Levinsohn wrote, some funders never ask themselves "what the cost might be to good and healthy organizations when [they] incentivize change over constancy. It sometimes seems that we take our best and most thoughtful practitioners and turn them into crazed hamsters on the spinning wheel of innovation."[12]

Erica Brown recently surveyed educational leaders to identify critical issues in the twenty-first century Jewish educational landscape. Her list of eighteen issues included the complaint that there are too many programs and not enough strategic thinking. "The organized Jewish community is too program-focused, said many respondents, with a tendency to 'diagnose problems and try to find the right program to solve them,'"[13] she wrote. "Investing in programs distracts us from investing in solid infrastructure and making the case for Jewish education generally." An organization is different from a program. It must have a sustainable and ongoing source of funds to maintain its infrastructure, seeking supplemental funding for its innovative work. But funding infrastructure, as everyone knows, is not as "sexy" as funding innovation or even renovation. Institutions need endowments that generate reliable revenue if they are to be sustainable; they can't live hand to mouth, scrambling each year to pay salaries and rent; fees for service do not generate sufficient revenue to reliably cover costs. When incredible results are not immediately forthcoming, will funders turn their attention elsewhere as they have been prone to do in the past?

Funders and entrepreneurs seek change and they want it yesterday. That is not how education works. Education, especially Jewish education, is a foundational effort that needs to persist over time to produce long-term results. Jewish education teaches knowledge and skills to young people who do not yet understand how they will apply to their lives in the future, but they must be learned and absorbed at an early age to become part of one's being and available when needed. This is what day schools do—lay a foundation day by day over years for the infrastructure of a life. There is no quick fix; this is nourishment, not inoculation. When funders and

12. Levinsohn, "Leadership," Para. 22.
13. Brown, "Reflecting," Para. 9.

Epilogue

community leaders place a disproportionate emphasis on programming instead of capacity building, they substitute immediate gratification for long-term benefits. This is short-sighted and has resulted in the failure of the American Jewish community at large to sustain itself. It must change. This is the most existential and important challenge Jewish federations have ever faced.

Jonathan Woocher advocated for a new learner-centered Jewish education in the twenty-first century, designed not for the goal of Jewish continuity but "to provide learners with the tools and resources to construct meaningful Jewish lives—understanding that these lives may not correspond to a preconceived image or norm, but will instead be unique 'remixes' of materials drawn from the multifarious storehouse of Jewish history and tradition and from other sources."[14] In this learner-centered paradigm, educators and learners are engaged in a partnership in which "Ultimately, it is about trusting learners to construct ways of being Jewish that work for them and accepting that these ways will be diverse and evolving."[15] Diversity and choice will be bywords for the Jewish community that exists outside of isolationist enclaves in the twenty-first century. At the same time, being Jewish means being part of a *community*. Jews were chosen as a *people*. Judaism is not a particularist faith but a communal one. Whether the Jewish people stand apart from the rest of society or whether they acculturate to it, to survive they must stand *together*. A Jew metaphorically must always be part of a *minyan*. That is what the Jewish community day school movement has always recognized and championed. In the twenty-first century, the Haredi world is moving toward greater stringency and isolation; the Reform and Conservative movements are struggling to define their core and their purpose; the Modern Orthodox world has yet to choose its direction. But the community day school world made its choices in the last century, and those choices were far-sighted and far-reaching.

Community is fundamental to the Jewish future. No longer is community geographically, socially, politically, or ethnically restricted. Community in the twenty-first century comprises the four basic elements identified by psychologists David W. McMillan and David M. Chavis: the feeling of belonging; the sense of mattering and of making a difference to a group; the feeling that members' needs will be met; and the belief that members have shared and will share history, common places, time together, and similar

---

14. Woocher, "Jewish Education," 206.
15. Woocher, "Jewish Education," 207.

experiences.[16] Over thirty-six years RAVSAK not only provided these elements of community to its own membership but extended them to other networks. Its strong emphasis on *Klal Yisrael* meant that it was open to partnerships, associations and working with others. In the JCDSN newsletter of September 1994, Chair Susan Cook emphasized this value: "The schools we head are really microcosms of the Jewish community at large, with all the attendant challenges and rewards. We bring together families of diverse levels of education and observance and attempt to create a school culture that reflects and respects that diversity, while being true to the traditions and values that bind us all. This is a difficult task, but made more difficult without the support of colleagues. So join with us. We will strengthen each other as we seek to strengthen our schools and our communities."

The day school as the nucleus of a Jewish future is not a new concept. Many of those who devoted their lives and careers to Jewish education have always known it to be true that only the immersive experience of a day school can provide young children and their families with the intellectual and social capital that can support a Jewish future in a secular world. Even the staunchest advocates of supplementary Jewish education, who held Americanization as one of their highest ideals, recognized this. A hundred years ago, Alexander Dushkin warned that "the Jewish parochial school program . . . is fraught with danger for America and the American Jew" since it aimed "to subject the Jewish child completely to Jewish influence . . . and the resultant sectarianism . . . may undermine the spirit of tolerance which is among America's proudest aims."[17] But fifty years later, he reversed his position, declaring that "In the years ahead it will be increasingly obligatory for Jewish educators to promote the establishment of day schools as the intensive core of the American Jewish school system."[18]

With the majority of American Jews several generations removed from their immigrant ancestors and far outstripping them in socioeconomic status, those who wish to see Judaism survive and thrive in the twenty-first century and beyond must recognize how precarious the Jewish future is right now. Without a critical mass of educated, committed, and knowledgeable young Jewish children and young adults, non-Haredi Judaism will not have a future in the United States. The barriers that once constrained Jews no longer exist. Jews now look, act, and achieve just like

---

16. McMillan and Chavis," Sense," 9.
17. Dushkin, *Jewish Education*, 48.
18. Dushkin and Engelman, *Jewish Education*, 207.

Epilogue

everybody else. As Steven Cohen cautioned, "Absent any effective intervention, fewer non-Orthodox Jews will be socialized into Jewish life; fewer will have been exposed to home observance, Jewish schooling, and other Jewish socialization experiences—largely because of the rising fraction of them who derive from mixed married homes. Put succinctly, non-Orthodox Jews will be numerically fewer and educationally thinner. As a result, engaged non-Orthodox Jews will contract, with direct adverse consequences for the entire organized Jewish communal infrastructure outside of Orthodoxy."[19] These are not warnings; they are predictive analytics.

For there to be a Jewish future, there needs to be an active commitment to Jewish community, identity, and values and practices that is not founded on rigidity, nostalgia, or guilt, but on a base of knowledge and a positive, proactive dedication to all that Judaism has stood for over the ages and all that it can continue to contribute for the benefit of humanity. A community day school can seed a Jewish community. It is no secret that Jewish organizations of all sorts are moribund; synagogue membership is graying and declining; JCCs serve multiple constituencies with significant non-Jewish participation; gender-based groups (sisterhoods, men's clubs) are passé. Jewish youth and young adults connect via social media more often than in person. But young families connect through their children. The Jewish community day school, even more than a preschool, gives a Jewish community a seven to twelve year opportunity to create *kehillot* (communities) of Jewish families who are connected through that which is most precious to them: their children.

Federations must provide sufficient financial support for community day schools to allow them a base line of superior academics, with fundraising devoted to providing the cutting-edge technology and sophisticated educational enhancements that will make Jewish parents proud, happy, and talking about how wonderful "their" day school is to everyone who will listen. Federations already know this. *A Time to Act* was written in 1990 but its words ring as true today as then: "In our uniquely pluralistic society, where there are so many philosophies and ideologies competing for attention, and where the pursuit of Judaism increasingly involves a conscious choice, the burden of preparation for such a decision resides with education. Jewish education must be compelling—emotionally, intellectually, and spiritually—so that Jews, young and old, will say to themselves: 'I have decided to remain engaged, to continue to investigate and grapple with these ideas,

---

19. Cohen, "Shrinking," 5–6.

and to choose an appropriate Jewish way of life.' Jewish education must be sustained, expanded, and vastly improved if it is to achieve this objective. It must become an experience that inspires greater numbers of Jews to learn, feel, and act in a way that reflects a deep understanding of Jewish values."[20]

The Jewish community day school is a vital portal to Jewish survival in a post-denominational, unaffiliated Jewish milieu. Faced with the myriad diversities of the modern world, Jewish community day schools opted to confront them squarely, fully embrace diversity and inclusivity, and be enriched and enlivened by differences. This is the only way the Jewish community can survive as a fully engaged, learned, and committed faith community in the twenty-first century. One can only hope that the leaders of the broader Jewish community can recognize how vital this model is to the future of Judaism in America, and can work to champion pluralism and *Klal Yisrael* as cherished Jewish and American values. As RAVSAK once proudly proclaimed: *Our client is the Jewish future.*

---

20. Commission on Jewish Education, *A Time to Act*, 26.

Bibliography

Ackerman, Walter I. "Jewish Education–For What?" *The American Jewish Year Book* 70 (1969) 3–36.

———. "Strangers to the Tradition: Ideas and Constraint in American Jewish Education." *Jewish Education World Wide*, (1990) 71–116.

Aiello, Barbara. "Pluralistic Judaism Unites Us All." http://rabbibarbara.com/pluralistic-judaism/.

American Jewish Committee. *Synagogue Council of America Records.* Collection archived at the American Jewish Historical Society. http://digifindingaids.cjh.org/?pID=109187.

Angel, Marc. "The Jewish Day School: A Symposium." *Tradition: A Journal of Orthodox Jewish Thought,* 32, 4 (Summer 1998), 24–27.

———"Thoughts on Modern Orthodox Jewish Life." https://www.jewishideas.org/article/thoughts-modern-orthodox-jewish-life.

Antin, Mary. *The Promised Land.* Mineola, NY: Dover Publications, 2012.

AVI CHAI Foundation. *Annual Report 2005.* New York: AVI CHAI Foundation, 2005.

Bayme, Steven. "Internal Jewish Cohesion: Problems and Prospects." *The Jewish People in the 21st Century,* (1998) 5–24.

———. *Jewish Arguments and Counterarguments: Essays and Addresses.* New York: KTAV, 2002.

Beinart, Peter. Review of *At Home in Exile* and *The Pious Ones.* https://www.nytimes.com/2014/11/09/books/review/at-home-in-exile-and-the-pious-ones.html.

Bennett, Daniel W. "A Community Day School Network." *The Pedagogic Reporter* (January 1988) 13–16.

Bieler, Jack. *Vision of a Modern Orthodox Education.* Jerusalem: Mandel Leadership Institute, 2008. https://my.mandelfoundation.org.il/mli_pdf/visions/bieler.pdf.

Bisk, Tsvi and Moshe Dror. "The Jewish Community of the 21st Century." http://www.onjewishmatters.com/the-jewish-community-of-the-21st-century/.

Boxer, Matthew. "The Myth of a Cohesive, United, American Jewish Community," https://forward.com/shma-now/al-tifrosh-min-hatzibur/351510/the-myth-of-a-cohesive-united-american-jewish-community/.

Brickman, William W. "The American Jewish Day School." *Tradition* 9 (Spring–Summer 1967) 176–193.

Brown, Erica. "Reflecting and Celebrating Conversations on Jewish Education." http://ejewishphilanthropy.com/reflecting-and-celebrating-conversations-

BIBLIOGRAPHY

on-jewish-education/?utm_source=March+5%2C+2018&utm_campaign=Mon+Mar+5&utm_medium=email.
Brumberg, Stephan F. *Going to America/Going to School*. New York: Praeger, 1986.
Bulka, Reuven. *The Coming Cataclysm*. Oakville, Ontario: Mosaic, 1986.
Chertok, Fern et al. *What Difference Does Day School Make: The Impact of Day School: A Comparative Analysis of Jewish College Students*. Boston, PEJE, 2007. http://hdl.handle.net/10192/22974.
Chipkin, Israel S. *Twenty-Five Years of Jewish Education in the United States*. New York: Jewish Education Association of New York City, 1937.
Cohen, Steven M. *The Impact of Varieties of Jewish Education upon Jewish Identity: An Inter-Generational Perspective*. Jerusalem: The Melton Centre for Jewish Education, 1995.
———. "Non-Denominational and Post Denominational." https://www.myjewishlearning.com/article/non-denominational-post-denominational/.
———. "The Shrinking Jewish Middle—And What to Do About It." http://hdl.handle.net/2027/spo.13469761.0027.001.
Commission on Jewish Education in North America. *A Time to Act*. New York: University Press of America, 1990.
Cooper, Bruce S. and Marc N. Kramer, "The New Jewish Community, New Jewish Schools: Trends and Promises." *Journal of Catholic Education*, 5 (4) 488–501. https://digitalcommons.lmu.edu/ce/vol5/iss4/5/.
Correspondent, J. "High tuition throttling day schools across U.S." https://www.jweekly.com/1997/10/24/high-tuition-throttling-day-schools-across-u-s/.
Covenant Foundation. *Award Brochure*. https://www.covenantfn.org/award-person/marc-kramer/.
Deen, Shulem. "Why Talmud Is the Way To Be Jewish Without Judaism." https://forward.com/my-heretical-year/342171/why-talmud-is-the-way-to-be-jewish-without-judaism/.
Drachler, Norman. *A Bibliography of Jewish Education in the United States*. Detroit: Wayne State University Press, 1996.
Drew, Glenn A. "The Delusion of Affordability." https://ejewishphilanthropy.com/the-delusion-of-affordability/.
Dushkin, Alexander M. *Jewish Education in New York City*. New York: Bureau of Jewish Education, 1918.
———. and Uriah Engleman. *Jewish Education in the United States*. New York: American Association for Jewish Education, 1959.
Edelstein, Abraham. "The Real Jewish Day School Crisis." http://www.aish.com/jw/s/The-Real-Jewish-Day-School-Crisis.html.
Edelstein, Shari L. Marcella Kanfer Rolnick and Yossi Prager. "Supporting Field Building Organizations." https://ejewishphilanthropy.com/supporting-field-building-organizations/.
El-Or, Tamar. *Educated and Ignorant: Ultraorthodox Jewish Women and Their World*. Boulder: Lynne Rienner, 1994.
Elazar, Daniel J. "Jewish Communal Structures Around the World." http://www.jcpa.org/dje/articles2/jewcommstruct.htm.
Ellenson, David. *The Future Of Jewish Education From The Reform Perspective: A Position Paper Submitted to the Jim Joseph Foundation*. New York: Hebrew Union College, 2006.

BIBLIOGRAPHY

English, Chuck. "Maximizing the Millennial Moment." *HaYidion* (Summer 2018) 10–12. https://prizmah.org/maximizing-millennial-moment-3.

Fishman, Deborah. "Rabbi Jonathan Sacks: 'If You Want to Save the Jewish Future, You Have to Build Jewish Day Schools.'" https://ejewishphilanthropy.com/rabbi-jonathan-sacks-if- you-want-to-save-the-jewish-future-you-have-to-build-jewish-day-schools/.

Fishman, Sylvia Barack. *The Way into the Varieties of Jewishness*. Woodstock: Jewish Lights, 2007.

Fleishman, Joel L. *First Annual Report to The AVI CHAI Foundation on the Progress of its Decision to Spend Down*. Duke University Sanford School of Public Policy, 2010.

Freedman, Samuel J. *Jew vs. Jew: The Struggle for the Soul of American Jewry*. New York: Simon & Schuster, 2000.

Gildiner, Rachel. "Strengthening Jewish Peoplehood through Relationships." http://www.bjpa.org/Publications/downloadFile.cfm?FileID=21336.

Glenn, Susan A. "The Jewish Cold War: Anxiety and Identity in the Aftermath of the Holocaust." http://quod.lib.umich.edu/b/belin/13469761.0024.001/—jewish-cold-war-anxiety-and-identity-in-the-aftermath?rgn=main;view=fulltext.

Goldhagen, Jonah. "The Lessons of Jewish Pluralism." https://forward.com/opinion/israel/154258/the-lessons-of-jewish-pluralism/.

Goldstein, Mark L. and Marilyn Forman Chandler. "Promoting Federation-Day School Collaboration to Address Sustainability in Smaller Communities." *HaYidion* (Summer 2004) 20–21. https://prizmah.org/promoting-federation-day-school-collaboration-address-sustainability-smaller-communities.

Gordon, Ken. "Seize the Day School." http://www.kveller.com/article/seize-the-day-school/.

———. "Turning to Day Schools When Synagogues Just Won't Do." https://forward.com/opinion/191415/turning-to-day-schools-when-synagogues-just-wont-d/.

Greenberg, Irving. "Will there be one Jewish people in the year 2000?" https://rabbiirvinggreenberg.com/wp-content/uploads/2013/02/Will-There-Be-One_red.pdf.

Greenberg, Yitz. "Can Modern Orthodoxy Be the New Center?" http://jewishweek.timesofisrael.com/can-modern-orthodoxy-be-the-new-center/.

Greene, Daniel. *The Jewish Origins of Cultural Pluralism*. Bloomington: Indiana University Press, 2011.

Gurock, Jeffrey S. *Orthodox Jews in America*. Bloomington: Indiana University Press, 2009.

Hanus, George. "Where Is Our Jewish Leadership Hiding?" http://www.aish.com/jw/s/48931972.html.

Harvey, Hal. "Why I Regret Pushing Strategic Philanthropy." https://docs.google.com/document/d/1gTovbS6wscMtXMeQYZa5TSFEomgwdlJoSrVCuAiLVMU/mobilebasic?pref=2&pli=1

Hasit, Arie. "In Defense of Jewish Pluralism." http://www.haaretz.com/jewish/the-jewish-thinker/in-defense-of-jewish-pluralism.premium-1.524892.

Heilman, Samuel C. *Defenders of the Faith*. New York: Schocken, 1992.

Herberg, Will. *Protestant, Catholic, Jew*. Chicago: University of Chicago Press, 1955.

Herring, Hayim. "Educating Rabbis for Jews without Borders." http://ejewishphilanthropy.com/educating-rabbis-for-jews-without-borders/.

Bibliography

Hertzberg, Arthur. "Assimilation." http://judaism_enc.enacademic.com/1486/ASSIMILATION

Himmelfarb, Milton. "In the light of Israel's victory." https://www.commentarymagazine.com/articles/in-the-light-of-israels-victory/.

Jerusalem Center for Public Affairs. "A Statement on Jewish Continuity." http://www.jcpa.org/dje/articles2/statement-contin.htm.

Jewish Women's Archive. "Ray Frank on Klal Yisrael." https://jwa.org/teach/golearn/sep05/youth.

Judd, Kate. "The Challenges of Jewish Pluralism." http://www.reformjudaism.org/blog/2013/06/18/challenges-jewish-pluralism.

Kallen, Horace. "Democracy Versus The Melting-Pot: A Study of American Nationality." *The Nation*, February 25, 1915. http://www.expo98.msu.edu/people/kallen.htm.

Kaminetsky, Joseph. "A Program for the Day School Movement In the '70's and Beyond." *Tradition* (Summer 1976) 120–126.

Kaplan, Mordechai. *Judaism as a Civilization: Toward a Reconstruction of American-Jewish Life*. Philadelphia: Jewish Publication Society, 1934.

Kaplan, Seth and Naftuli Moster. "Why Do Jewish Leaders Keep Ignoring Ultra-Orthodox Education Crisis?" http://forward.com/opinion/341055/why-do-jewish-leaders-keep-ignoring-ultra-orthodox-education-crisis/#ixzz4CEk8xpnQ.

Kaplan, Shmuel. "Jewish Religious Pluralism Is a Destructive Idea." http://jewishweek.timesofisrael.com/jewish-religious-pluralism-is-a-destructive-idea/.

Kardos, Susan. "Who's Who at AVI CHAI." http://avichai.org/2012/08/whos-who-at-avi-chai-featuring-dr-susan-m-kardos/.

Kay, Michael. "The Paradox of Pluralism: Diversity as the Foundation for Community." http://jdov.org/talk/the-paradox-of-pluralism-diversity-as-the-foundation-of-community/.

———. "Threefold Pluralism: A Strategy for Building 'Hybrid' School Community." *HaYidion* (Winter 2009) 3–8. https://prizmah.org/threefold-pluralism-strategy-building-%E2%80%9Chybrid%E2%80%9D-school-community.

Kimelman, Reuven. "Judaism and Pluralism." *Modern Judaism* 7 (1987) 131–50. http://www.jstor.org/stable/1396236.

Kramer, Mark N. "A Few Thoughts on Jewish Diversity." *HaYidion* (Autumn 2007) 12–15. https://prizmah.org/few-thoughts-jewish-diversity.

———. "Jewish Literacy Empowers Jewish Action." https://ejewishphilanthropy.com/jewish-literacy-empowers-jewish-action/.

———. "Teaching in a Jewish Community School." In *The Ultimate Jewish Teacher's Handbook*, edited by Nachama Skolnik Moskowitz, 66–72. Springfield, NJ: A.R.E., 2003.

Krasner, Jonathan. "Between Universalism and Particularism: Rethinking the Teaching of Jewish History." *HaYidion* (Spring 2016) 17–18. https://prizmah.org/between-universalism-and-particularism-rethinking-teaching-jewish-history.

LaPiana, David. *Real Collaboration: A Guide for Grantmakers*. New York: Ford Foundation, 2001. http://bjseminars.com.au/real-collaboration/.

Lehmann, Daniel. "The Promise of Community High Schools." In *The Jewish Educational Leader's Handbook*, edited by Robert E. Tornberg, 606–620. Springfield, NJ: A.R.E., 1998.

BIBLIOGRAPHY

———. "Beyond Continuity, Identity, and Literacy." *HaYidion* (August 2014) 10–17. https://prizmah.org/beyond-continuity-identity-and-literacy-making-compelling-case-jewish-day-schools-21st-century.

Levinsohn, Jon A. "Leadership Fast and Slow." *HaYidion* (Winter 2018) 71–73.https://prizmah.org/leadership-fast-and-slow.

———. "Ideas and Ideals of Jewish Education: Initiating a Conversation on *Visions of Jewish Education.*" *Journal of Jewish Education*, 71 (2005) 53–66.

Librach, Clifford. "Does Conservative Judaism Have a Future?" https://www.commentarymagazine.com/articles/does-conservative-judaism-have-a-future/.

Linsky, Marty. "The Future of Reform Judaism: How Can We Lead in Challenging Times?" http://blogs.rj.org/blog/2015/10/20/the-future-of-reform-judaism-how-can-we-lead-in-challenging-times/.

Lipman, Steve. "Day School Groups Merge in Big Educational Shakeup." http://www.thejewishweek.com/news/new-york/day-school-groups-merge-big-educational-shakeup.

Lorch, Stephen. "Pluralism: An Inquiry." *HaYidion* (Autumn 2014) 26–28. https://prizmah.org/pluralism-inquiry.

Magid, Shaul. "Pluralism, Ethos, Creativity and Israel." *HaYidion* (August 2014) 28–30. https://prizmah.org/pluralism-ethos-creativity-and-israel.

Malkus, Mitchell. "Can We Attract the Majority of American Jews to Day Schools?" https://ejewishphilanthropy.com/can-we-attract-the-majority-of-american-jews-to-day-schools/.

———. "What defines a pluralistic Jewish school?" https://blogs.timesofisrael.com/what-defines-a-pluralistic-jewish-school/.

Mansour, Eli. "Reheating Foods on Shabbat Containing Congealed Fat." http://www.dailyhalacha.com/displayRead.asp?readID=2991.

McMillan, David W. and David M. Chavis. "Sense of community: a definition and theory." *Journal of Community Psychology*, 1 (1986) 6–23.

Miller, Josh. "A New Experiment in National-Local Funder Collaboration." https://ejewishphilanthropy.com/a-new-experiment-in-national-local-funder-collaboration/.

Moses, Jay Henry. "Learning Opportunity: Collaboration Won't Kill Us, but Failing to Collaborate Might." In *Moving to the Leading Edge*, 23–4. New York: Union for Reform Judaism, 2016. http://www.urj.org/sites/default/files/MovingtotheLeadingEdge.pdf.

Nathan-Kazis, Jonathan. "Can New President Ari Berman Save Yeshiva University?" https://forward.com/news/350522/can-new-president-ari-berman-save-yeshiva-university/.

———. "Where Are All the Non-Orthodox Rabbis?." Forward, February 18, 2015. https://forward.com/news/214663/where-are-all-the-non-orthodox-rabbis/.

North American Commission on Jewish Identity and Continuity. *To Renew and Sanctify: A Call to Action*. New York: Council of Jewish Federations, 1995.

Oz, Amos. *Jewsandwords*. New Haven: Yale University Press, 2012.

The Pluralism Project. "Judaism in America." http://pluralism.org/timeline/judaism-in-america/.

———. "The Challenge of Assimilation." http://pluralism.org/religions/judaism/issues-for-jews-in-america/the-challenge-of-assimilation/.

Bibliography

Pomson, Alex. "Jewish Schools, Jewish Communities: A Reconsideration." In *Jewish Day Schools, Jewish Communities*, edited by Alex Pomson and Howard Deitcher, 1–30, Oxford: Littman Library of Jewish Civilization, 2009.

Pruzansky, Steven. "An Exchange." https://rabbipruzansky.com/2014/03/14/an-exchange/.

Rabbinical Council of America. "Patrilineal Descent," June 1, 1983, http://www.rabbis.org/news/article.cfm?id=101084 .

———. "RCA Passes Resolution Regarding Ordination of Women," October 30, 2015, http://www.rabbis.org/news/article.cfm?id=105836 .

———. "RCA Policy Concerning Women Rabbis," October 31, 2015. http://www.rabbis.org/news/article.cfm?id=105835

———. "Response to Rabbinical Assembly's Decisions Regarding Ordination of Gays and Lesbians, and "Commitment Ceremonies," Dec 7, 2006, http://www.rabbis.org/news/article.cfm?id=100869.

Rayner, John D. *Affirmations of Liberal Judaism*. London: Union of Liberal and Progressive Synagogues, 2006.

RAVSAK. *Our Client is the Jewish Future: 10 Year Review*. New York: RAVSAK, 2010.

Reimer, Joseph. *Succeeding at Jewish Education: How One Synagogue Made it Work*. Philadelphia: Jewish Publication Society, 1997.

Ruskay, John. *Historical Change and Communal Responsibility: The Jewish Communal Agenda and the Challenge of Emerging Philanthropic Trends*. New York: UJA/Federation of Jewish Philanthropies, 1996.

Ruskay, John S. and Alisa Rubin Kurshan. "American Jewry's Focus on Continuity at Ten Years." *Journal of Jewish Communal Service* (Fall/Winter 1999) 81–88.

Sacks, Jonathan. *The Dignity of Difference: How to Avoid the Clash of Civilizations*. London: Continuum, 2002.

Sales, Amy L. *Philanthropic Lessons from Mapping Jewish Education*. Boston: Fisher-Bernstein Institute for Jewish Philanthropy and Leadership, 2007.

Salmon, Felix. "Philanthropy: You're doing it wrong." http://blogs.reuters.com/felix-salmon/2012/12/25/philanthropy-youre-doing-it-wrong/.

Sarna, Jonathan D. "American Jewish Education in Historical Perspective." *Journal of Jewish Education*, 64:1–2 (Winter/Spring) 1998, 8–21.

———. *American Jews in the New Millennium*. Waltham, MA: Brandeis University, 1999. https://www.brandeis.edu/hornstein/sarna/contemporaryjewishlife/Archive/AmericanJewsintheNewMillenium.pdf.

Schick, Marvin. *A Census of Jewish Day Schools in the United States*. New York: AVI CHAI Foundation, 2000.

———. *A Census of Jewish Day Schools in the United States 2003–2004*. New York: AVI CHAI Foundation, 2005.

———. *A Census of Jewish Day Schools in the United States 2008–2009*. New York: AVI CHAI Foundation, 2009.

Schiff, Alvin I. *The Jewish Day School in America*. New York: Jewish Education Committee, 1968.

Seymour, Jack L. and Elizabeth Caldwell. Preface to Sarah M. Tauber, *Open Minds, Devoted Hearts: Portraits of Adult Religious Educators*. Eugene: Pickwick, 2015.

Shapiro, Edward S. *A Time for Healing: American Jewry since World War II*. Baltimore: Johns Hopkins University Press, 1992.

BIBLIOGRAPHY

———. "The Crisis of Conservative Judaism: Conservative Jews Face Decline and Division." https://www.firstthings.com/article/2013/05/the-crisis-of-conservative-judaism.

Shapiro, Rami. "My Response to 'A Portrait of Jewish Americans.'" https://www.tikkun.org/nextgen/rami-shapiro-responds-to-the-pew-report-on-american-jewry.

Sheramy, Rona. "The Day School Tuition Crisis: A Short History." https://jewishreviewofbooks.com/articles/511/the-day-school-tuition-crisis-a-short-history/.

Shostak, Eddie. "To School or To Shul? That is the Question: Twenty-five Minutes in a Car with Rabbi Lord Jonathan Sacks." http://ejewishphilanthropy.com/to-school-or-to-shul-that-is-the-question-twenty-five-minutes-in-a-car-with-rabbi-lord-jonathan-sacks/.

Siegel, Jennifer. "Will Conservative Day Schools Survive?" https://forward.com/news/13533/will-conservative-day-schools-survive-01977/.

Slingshot '07–08. https://www.slingshotfund.org/organizations/?q=ravsak.

Steinhardt, Michael. "Day Schools Should Emphasize Secular Education." https://jewishweek.timesofisrael.com/day-schools-should-emphasize-secular-education/.

Strassfeld, Michael. "The Open Society." https://www.thesaj.org/articles.

Tabachnik, Toby. "Old Models of Jewish Legacy Institutions No Longer Working, Experts Say." https://ejewishphilanthropy.com/old-models-of-jewish-legacy-institutions-no-longer-working-experts-say/.

Wachs, Saul. "Devar Torah presented to the Gratz College Board of Governors, Tishrei 5776." https://gratzcommunityblog.wordpress.com/2015/09/21/devar-torah-presented-by-dr-saul-wachs-to-the-gratz-college-board-of-governors-september-20-2015-tishrei-7-5776/.

Wasserfall, Rahel and Susan L. Shevitz. "Building Community in a Pluralist Jewish High School: Balancing Risk and Safety, Group and Individual in the Life of a School." http://www.brandeis.edu/mandel/pdfs/PluralismBuildingCommunity072109.pdf.

Weintrob, Susan. "From The Desk of Susan Weintrob, RAVSAK President," *HaYidion* (Autumn 2007) 3. https://prizmah.org/desk-susan-weintrob-ravsak-president.

Weiss, Avi and Rella Fellman. "A More Inclusive Modern Orthodoxy." http://www.tabletmag.com/scroll/202196/a-more-inclusive-modern-orthodoxy.

Jack Wertheimer, ed. *Imagining the Jewish Community.* Waltham, MA: Brandeis University Press, 2007.

———. "Jews and the Jewish Birthrate." http://www.aish.com/jw/s/48899452.html.

———, ed. *Tradition Renewed: A History of the Jewish Theological Seminary.* New York: Jewish Theological Seminary of America, 1997.

———, and Manfred Gerstenfeld. "The Future of Jewish Education: An interview with Jack Wertheimer." In *American Jewry's Comfort Level: Present and Future,* 201–210. Jerusalem Center for Public Affairs, 2010. https://www.bjpa.org/search-results/publication/8260

Winshall, Arnee. "From the Desk of Arnee Winshall." *HaYidion,* (Summer 2013), 6. https://prizmah.org/desk-arnee-winshall-ravsak-chair-9.

Wolpe, David. "The Chief Rabbi's Achievement." http://jewishreviewofbooks.com/articles/234/the-chief-rabbis-achievement.

Woocher, Jonathan S. "Foreword" to Joseph Reimer, *Succeeding at Jewish Education: How One Synagogue Made It Work.* Lincoln: University of Nebraska Press, 1997.

———. "Jewish Education: From Continuity to Meaning." In *Jewish Megatrends.* Woodstock, 202–18, VT: Jewish Lights, 2013.

www.ingramcontent.com/pod-product-compliance
Lightning Source LLC
Chambersburg PA
CBHW060823190426
43197CB00038B/2206